Managing Public Services

Managing Public Services

Competition and decentralization

Richard Common
Norman Flynn
and
Elizabeth Mellon

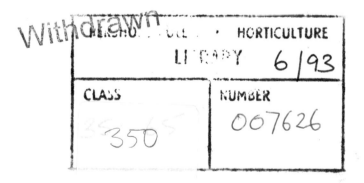

BUTTERWORTH
HEINEMANN

Butterworth-Heinemann Ltd
Linacre House, Jordan Hill, Oxford OX2 8DP

PART OF REED INTERNATIONAL BOOKS

OXFORD LONDON BOSTON
MUNICH NEW DELHI SINGAPORE SYDNEY
TOKYO TORONTO WELLINGTON

First published 1992
First published as a paperback edition 1993

British Library Cataloguing in Publication Data
Common, Richard
    Managing public services.
    I. Title.   II. Flynn, Norman   III. Mellon, Elizabeth
    350

ISBN 0 7506 0977 X

Typeset by MS Filmsetting Ltd, Frome, Somerset
Printed and bound in Great Britain by
Biddles Ltd, Guildford and King's Lynn

Contents

Foreword

It is with pleasure and a sense of honour that I introduce *Managing Public Services: Competition and Decentralization*. Rarely can a work have been so much needed by a sector pressured into widespread changes. These changes have been less tested and worked through than debated and voted through by the larger of three organized minorities, facing a rhetorical opposition, from the far side of an ideological divide. It would be surprising under such circumstances for the best of all public services to emerge.

What we seem to have is something akin to a free association around the words 'private sector', 'competition', 'decentralization' and 'customer service'. It was as if the public services, by rubbing shoulders with these more esteemed characters, would be exposed to reformative influences. It is to the credit of the public sector managers described in this book, that despite being issued with such conceptual small arms, and with little training in their use, they have wrought the many improvements detailed in these pages. It is a triumph of improvisation over inadequate policy. After a decade in which public service has almost become the equivalent of a 'national burden', infected with 'sloth', the many sustained efforts to do a better job with one's remaining staff shine through these chapters.

The problem really begins with the notion of profit. This is something to which the private sector pays close attention, along with what used to be called 'the Free World'. Organizations and economies not steered by profitability seem to have had a very patchy record and are finding it increasingly difficult to justify their continued existence. So today we all believe in profit.... Unfortunately the word means many different things, from the triumph of self-interest to the doom of any endeavour built upon an ideal of public service. Adam Smith's scorn sounds to us over the centuries.

> By pursuing his own interest he frequently promotes that of society more effectually than when he really intends to promote it. I have never known much good done by those who affected to trade in the public good.

My own view of profitability, which I believe the authors share, is that it works very well in most, if not all, parts of the private sector because it *reconciles key existential dilemmas*. For example, profitability rewards *individuals* in accordance with their success in the *social* task of satisfying customers, thereby turning *public* satisfactions into *private* gains commensurate to that satisfaction. It sponsors *competition* in who can best *cooperate* to produce goods and service customers, moving more and more resources towards those who do this best and away from those who do this poorly.

So far from profitability representing the triumph of the individual, of the private sector and of competition *over* social obligation, public concern and cooperative ideals, profitability is the *reconciler* of such values, the best indicator we have that synergy has been achieved among 'opposed' objectives. This view helps to explain the economic successes of Germany, Japan and 'the Five Dragons' of the Pacific Rim. In all these countries business is regarded as much more of a public service and social duty than among English speaking nations. All fast-developing nations are profit oriented but *not* individually competitive or enthusiastic about maximizing private gain. This 'Confucian Dynamic' is communitarian and pro-production rather than consumerist.

Now profit-as-a-reconciler is generally unavailable to the public sector for many reasons ably set out in this book. It is unacceptable, for example, to give the rich superior access to public services. In many cases the service is there to regulate the public, not to please it; to educate and inform, not to entertain. All public services have *at least* two constituencies, sometimes many more – those originating policies and those receiving them. Their aims, to put it mildly, are frequently at odds.

The answer that each public service needs to find is a *measure of reconciliation equivalent to that of profit in the private sector*, and for each service that calculation will be different because its dilemmas are different. Each needs to find unique ways of estimating and measuring seemingly 'opposed' objectives, i.e. saving the Treasury and the taxpayer on the delivery of medical care *and* serving the public effectively and expeditiously. It would be a simple idea indeed to care extravagantly and let costs rip, or to pinch pennies, lengthen waiting lists and drive desperate patients into private care. What is required of the NHS and health policy is a difficult balancing act – cost effective, high quality care.

It comes as a pleasant surprise in reading this book to discover the extent to which public sector managers have intuited these 'double binds' and in some cases have achieved the best of both worlds. We have much to learn from these examples, meanings snatched from seeming conflicts of aims.

To a large extent we have inherited the hopelessness that many feel about 'bureaucracy'. Max Weber taught us that civil servants were rational actors or agents of policies decreed by governments. While politicians can be colourful, passionate, power-seeking, visionary, idealistic or occasionally mad, the civil servant administers such policies with a bloodless and detached precision, making sure that consequences flow logically from premises, that effects follow causes and that information remains neutral and objective.

This ideal of public service has never been a very attractive one, although it was until quite recently respected with 'picked, clever, young people' recruited from top universities. Where civil servants become the mere means to ends devised by others it becomes fatally easy to claim that they are inefficient instruments, means that have become ends in themselves, grey armies of *apparatchiks* seeking to perpetuate themselves at taxpayers' expense. Policies are not mistaken but are *badly and expensively delivered*. Acording to this view public services should be more akin to Sainsbury's or Marks and Spencer – 'decentralized', 'competitive', 'close to the customer' with managers 'walking about' and, in the words of the authors, 'playing at shops'.

What is worrying in this separation of policy from agency is the tendency to blame agents for failures of policy and for the mounting costs of services. This disconnection tends to hide the realities of mixed messages and divided allegiances. In what sense can a Vehicle Inspectorate 'please' its customers when its job is to keep those with unsafe vehicles off the road? Can a school or hospital 'compete' for patients or pupils when its mandate includes accessibility to all, especially the disadvantaged and most ill? Why *wouldn't* such institutions compete in shedding their more costly and intractable customers? These are problems of policy not of distribution, issues of effectiveness not efficiency. The public services have become the classic case of 'the man in the middle' blamed for not serving the public adequately with severely rationed resources. The danger is that public services will come to resemble the notorious Fenchurch Street line on which furious commuters expend impotent anger.

To be truly effective government policies need to be reality-tested by the public service which is appropriate. The danger lies in the political expedient of blaming the test instead of the policy. This is not to deny that economies in delivery can be made, or that those who serve the public, even in regulatory roles, cannot do so more skilfully and helpfully. This book is full of such examples, but even here such simplistic injunctions as 'decentralize' and 'get closer to customers' are of very limited range and usefulness.

Effective organizations in the private sector are not 'more decentralized' they are 'more decentralized *and better centralized*' for the simple reason that the more 'nerve endings' you extend into the environment the more complex must become the 'nerve centre' that has to coordinate these: the interdependence of centralizing and decentralizing is a biological truism. So what we have here is yet another dilemma. Decentralizing can, like centralizing, be taken too far, allowing a public service extension to be captured by its constituency. Among regulatory agencies the interface with customers is usually the source of irregularities and corruption. Only if the ratio of centralization to decentralization is just right can *information arising from interface with customers feed back to the centre to alter policy.*

What it ultimately comes down to is the capacity to steer towards chosen objectives and learn in the process of acting how to improve the *indivisible wholeness* of policy and delivery. Profitability usually allows organizations in the private sector to steer between 'horns of dilemmas'. Organizations in the public sector can only gain equivalent advantages by asking: 'what are our dilemmas?' Even where these are in tension or mutually impeding, like cost and quality, 'can we chart progress on both measures'. This book gives many incisive examples of how such dual challenges have been confronted and managed.

Charles Hampden-Turner
The Judge Centre
Cambridge University

Acknowledgements

We would like to express our appreciation to all the people who gave up their time to answer our questions and to Alexis, Gus Barnett, Patrick Dunleavy, David Falcon, George Jones, Stephanie Macauley, Tim Morris, Nigel Nicholson, Julian Rizello and Ellie Scrivens for their comments on the first draft. We would also like to acknowledge the financial assistance of the Leverhulme Trust and the Economic and Social Research Council.

1 Introduction

'Shoddy public services are not an option.'
The Rt Hon John Major MP

This is a book primarily for those public sector managers who have lived through the reforms of the last dozen or so years and who are still attempting to grapple with their consequences. Our aim is to step back from the individual initiatives and try to make sense of the whole. We seek to help public sector managers assess the position they find themselves in today, in order to assist them to think creatively about different approaches for the future.

The various initiatives which were undertaken in the public sector during the 1980s have one general principle underlying them: business is good, bureaucracy is bad. Business was, in the Conservative model, no longer to be subsidized, but to become independent. The Department of Trade and Industry, for example, no longer had Sponsor Divisions looking after different industries (and arranging subventions for investment), but Market Divisions, to promote trade and investment, but no longer to subsidize it. Old industries would not be allowed to continue to under-utilize capital and labour: they should be allowed to fade to make way for more vigorous market competitors. The Government would play its part by reducing inflation and helping industry to export through sound economic policies. Industry would thus become sharper, leaner and more efficient.

Public sector bureaucracy, on the other hand, was too big, too conservative, too politicized and too wasteful. Therefore some of it should be sold so that it would become subject to the rigours of the revitalized market place. What could not be sold would be reformed.

Reforms of the machinery of government have developed a variety of mechanisms with which to control the institutions of the public sector. Organizations such as government departments, non-departmental public bodies, local and health authorities are not susceptible to direct rule through instructions. Some are under more direct control than others but all retain degrees of autonomy through professionalism, popular support or sheer inertia. All the levers which have been developed have been associated with 'management' in some form or other.

The simplest lever consisted of a process of clarifying the activities and then measuring the organizations' performance. Sometimes this was accompanied, especially in the Civil Service, by some form of 'management by objectives'. Hence public expenditure plans are published along with measures of performance through which managers can be held accountable. Simple measurements, such as unit costs or volume of activity enabled comparisons to be made among organizations. These comparisons then produced standards against which managers could be judged. Questions such as, 'why does it cost your unit twice as much as the average to produce a unit of output?' could then be directed at managers.

To enable these questions to be asked more systematically, bodies such as the National Audit Office were given wider remits, the Audit Commission was set up to review local authority performance (and later the performance of the NHS) and select committees of the House of Commons, especially the Treasury and Civil Service Select Committee, took a greater interest in questions of performance.

A Financial Management Initiative was pursued within the Civil Service to establish units of accountability and systems for measuring their performance, especially spending. Its purpose was to allow managers and, ultimately, ministers to know more about what was going on and to exercise more control over it.

All these mechanisms were attempts to expose costs and other elements of performance to public scrutiny but apart from moral pressure there was no consistent attempt to modify managers' behaviour. If performance is exposed but there are neither rewards nor sanctions for managers it is not obvious that the measurement will make any difference. Other initiatives did include structural changes which were supposed to lead to modified behaviour by managers. The division of many Civil Service departments into policy divisions and service-delivery agencies was such a move. Responsibility for managing services was supposed to be separated from the task of advising ministers. Those who were put in charge of the agencies were given targets and financial incentives to meet them. Clarity of objectives combined with a financial incentive was expected to produce appropriate managerial behaviour in a way in which public exposure of performance had not.

At a more radical level, the separation of policy from service delivery was extended to a separation of organizations into 'buyers' and 'sellers' or 'purchasers' and 'providers' through the establishment of internal markets. This approach was applied in the National Health Service, in personal social services and in some parts of the civil service. Even without setting up competition among 'providers' the division of the organization and the establishment of a financial transaction is supposed to expose costs and to expose managers to scrutiny.

Decentralization, or the attempt to break up organizations into smaller, more accountable units, was also an attempt to hold managers more accountable for the performance of their units of the organization. Large parts of central government departments were divided into Policy units and Executive Agencies whose task is to deliver services. Two principles underlying the Executive Agency initiative in central Government were of structural reorganization to enable the service delivery functions of Government to operate more effectively, and of '... radical change in the freedom to manage ...' (Efficiency Unit, 1988) so that substantially better results could be achieved. Professors Christopher Hood and George Jones of the Public Policy Group at the London School of Economics argue that 'corporatization' (the breaking up of a formerly unitary organization into units with separate identity and a degree of management autonomy) '... is contestable in that there is no real consensus of academic and professional opinion on the effects of corporatization ... The programme is built on promise in that, like most managerial doctrines, it rests on the bureaucratic equivalent of "market sentiment", not on hard evidence that corporatization "delivers"' (Evidence to the Treasury and Civil Service Select Committee, HMSO, July 1990).

Managers within the Executive Agencies certainly interpret their change in status as the Government's attempt to make them more 'business-like', or bringing market pressures to bear. While fewer believe that the initiative is any longer a pseudonym, like earlier initiatives, for cutting staff numbers, many still believe it is a step along the route to privatization. One attraction of the agency concept is rooted in the managerialist approach of decentralization and comes from the idea that it is the nearest the government can get to placing an organization at arm's length from itself.

Even more radical has been the exposure of managers to competition. In local authorities, managers of services such as building, highway construction and maintenance, street cleaning, catering etc. were forced to compete for contracts with private companies (Walsh, 1991). NHS hospitals now compete with each other and with private hospitals for patients. The National Health Service and Community Care Act 1990 in effect has meant that social services departments' own provision is in competition with alternative providers. Before it was put up for sale, the Property Services Agency, which looks after government estates, was put into competition with private builders. Some of the Executive Agencies are in competition with other people for all or part of their income. Competition was supposed to produce a downward pressure on costs as managers and workers competed to keep their jobs.

Accompanying this introduction of competitive pressure has been an increased use of performance related pay for managers. Workers have been subject to performance bonuses in the public sector for twenty years or more but it has been a new phenomenon for some managers. Short-term contracts with a proportion of the reward based on the organization's performance has been used as a further lever with which to control managers.

A recent lever has been the strengthening of consumer power. The Citizen's Charter, for example, is an attempt to squeeze managers from the bottom while they are also being pressured from above.

These mechanisms are all relatively simple to operate. However, they have been accompanied by a rhetoric which has claimed that they add up to a managerial revolution. As the economy emerged from the recession at the beginning of the 1980s there developed a cult of tough management, especially 'turnaround' management which took radical measures to save companies which were almost killed by the recession. Turnaround managers were ruthless in cost-cutting, imaginative in spotting new products and markets, and single minded in the pursuit of profits. What the public sector needed, according to the Government and its, mainly accountant, advisers was a similar breed. A 'new breed of manager' would sweep aside bureaucracy, would manage in a 'business-like' way, would establish real 'bottom line' management and so on. Since the private sector knew best, the public sector should learn from it and imitate its methods, or at least adopt its language. Hence, as we shall see, even if there were no competition managers would talk about beating the opposition. Even if the accounting systems were such that making a profit were a paper exercise, managers would emphasize the importance of the bottom line. Even if the organization's task did not involve generating revenue, managers would talk about 'running an £x million business'.

One consequence of the initiatives was that it allowed ministers to identify those matters for which they were not accountable. For example, in April 1991, the NHS Hospital Trust which runs Guy's Hospital and Lewisham General Hospital announced that it was to reduce the numbers of staff by 800 to enable the Trust to meet its expenditure target. Only three weeks after its establishment, the Trust had begun the process of changing its cost structure. It also announced that was to re-orient its services, dropping some of those activities which are uncompetitive and concentrating on those through which it could compete either on price or on quality. William Waldegrave was questioned about the announcement and said that the detailed management of the Trusts should be left to their Boards. Competitive forces would determine the outcome of the introduction of the internal market. It had always been an illusion that the provision of healthcare could be planned effectively in detail by the Department of Health.

The 'market' solution is very attractive for governments: the outcomes of competition are the result of the 'unseen hand' of the market, rather than the very visible hand of individual ministers. High cost providers have tended to be those hospitals which are old and famous and are staffed, in part, by powerful members of the medical establishment. Lobbying and public campaigning is replaced by market competition as the main strategy for survival.

The most radical lever, privatization, has been well researched, especially by Bishop and Kay (1988). They describe privatization as an accidental policy, devised before 1979, while the Conservatives were in opposition, as a means of reducing the power of public sector trade unions, and as a marginal policy in the early years. 'Over the years of Conservative Government since 1979, privatization has grown from a potential (and, in practice, little used) instrument of labour market reform, into the Government's central microeconomic policy ... The growth of privatization into a central feature of the Government's political programme had rather different origins. British Telecom ... planned a substantial investment programme based on the introduction of electronic switching ... the Government had chosen to base its macroeconomic policies on a Medium Term Financial Strategy in which targets for public sector borrowing played a central role. There was much discussion of mechanisms by which the funding of telecommunications investment could be excluded from calculations of the public sector borrowing requirement (PSBR). The conclusion of this arcane theological dispute was that no mechanism existed. This paved the way for the radical decision to transform British Telecom into a private company' (Bishop and Kay, 1988).

This 'accidental' policy soon blossomed and privatization of British Gas, British Airways, Rolls-Royce and others soon followed. People who favoured privatization as a policy saw different advantages in it. Apart from the original intention to reduce the power of public sector trade unions, it was also applauded because it diminished the PSBR, it created wider share ownership and because it was supposed to increase the efficiency of the privatized companies, once they were exposed to the rigours of the market place. There was, as Bishop and Kay argue, '... a loosely argued ideological faith in the superiority of private ownership'. There has never, therefore, been one rationale for a privatization policy and indeed the motives and justifications used have changed over time. 'Value for money' represents just one of these.

Bishop and Kay have tried carefully to assess the gains from privatization. They concluded that, 'All the industries concerned have registered substantial productivity gains ...' and that 'Quality has not fallen – social objectives continue to be pursued.' However, he adds two qualifications. The first is that, although privatized industries have tended to be faster growing and more profitable, it is this that leads to their privatization, rather than that they achieve this because of privatization. Secondly, and even more importantly, growth in productivity appears to be wholly unrelated to privatization, because productivity gains are variable and equalled or excelled by industries either not privatized or privatized later. As Bishop and Kay say '... and the poorest performance since 1983 comes from the flagship of privatization, British Telecom.'

However, even though the idea that private ownership and market solutions produce more favourable results is contested, it is interesting to consider how this belief has tempered and shaped policies enacted for public sector business. We therefore try in this book to assess the success of the policy measures undertaken for those parts of the public sector which have been reformed while remaining in public ownership.

As the head of the Home Civil Service, Sir Robin Butler, said in his lecture to the Institute of Personnel Management on 20 September 1988, 'Under the present Government the application of competition and of market discipline has been greatly extended. But there remain large areas of government activity which cannot be made subject to a commercial regime. That is why the Civil Service has invested a good deal of time and effort producing other mechanisms for evaluating performance.' He may have underestimated the degree to which commercial style disciplines have been applied even in those parts of the public sector which have remained in public ownership.

In this book we are mainly concerned with two levers for change which have been developed: structural change through decentralization both to and within organizations, and the introduction of competition.

It is often difficult to discern what differences a policy change has made to the internal processes and procedures of Government Departments and other public services. Partly the secrecy (usually termed 'confidentiality') surrounding the implementation of many Government initiatives makes any assessment difficult. Also, however, a policy general enough to work its way through two Houses of Parliament while satisfying some common denominator interest of both ministers and back benchers (opposition parties have been hard put to influence policy since 1979) is often broad in its recommendations for implementation. This leaves a lot of scope for 'bounded rationality' and 'routinization' to decrease the impact of changes. By this we mean that individuals can consider only a limited number of options and that the necessity of applying policies across widely varying circumstances can lead to the means to achieve the policy becoming ends in themselves. For example, in one light, the list of existing and potential Executive Agencies makes impressive reading because it is 78 long (as of July 1991: see Appendix I) and covers some 230 000 staff. The Civil Servant in charge of implementing the initiative, Sir Peter Kemp, states vehemently that this initiative is not about 'badge engineering' i.e. changing the name while the content remains the same. In another light, however, if producing Agencies has become a target in itself, rather than producing new forms of organization which make a real difference, then the initiative can hardly be termed a success. It is just such an assessment which this book contains.

For our assessment to be of use, we need to think carefully about a definition of 'success'. The first question is whose definition of success is important? The government as a whole may pursue many agendas and therefore many success criteria. The Treasury is primarily concerned with saving money. Ministers may be content if the initiatives reduce their exposure to blame which is deflected onto managers. However, in some cases government departments have established clear and measurable success criteria.

Managers themselves are developing their own managerial agenda. Even if the growth of managerial ideas takes place at the level of rhetoric, people who have been hired to do a managerial job expect to be able to manage. The culture of management has taken root in all the organizations we looked at. The satisfactions from work for managers include power, discretion, financial reward and in many cases the ability to do a good job and provide good services. They will judge the reforms by the degree to which they are able to achieve these satisfactions.

The users of services have different criteria, which involve the ability to get good services and whether they have choice and control over the services they receive.

Our first criterion is that the initiative should have made some measurable difference to the performance of the organizations, as defined by the people who put the reforms in train.

Our second criterion is that the initiative should have made some difference to the way people think about their work. Measurement is harder, in that collating subjective views is more challenging than amassing lists of documented changes. However, it is a useful and necessary adjunct to documented changes. To put it crudely, if I have been given more responsibility but feel that I have no more responsibility, I will continue to act according to old rules and customs and there will be no measurable difference in what I produce or the way in which I produce it. More importantly, I will feel that no changes have been made and to be faced with 'evidence' to the contrary will exacerbate my feelings of frustration and cynicism. This criterion is therefore crucial as a reality check to ensure that 'means' have not become 'ends'.

The third criterion is that users or customers should perceive in the long term some difference, for better or worse. The latter proviso is necessary because, when organizations first start to talk about improvements to service delivery, customer expectations can be raised above any level that can be achieved in the short term. Therefore, subjective measures of improvement from customers can show deterioration in service in the short term. There is also a time-lag effect: customers take time to notice any changes, having been conditioned to one level of service. If customers perceive no difference in the longer run, one has to ask whether the initiative has any point, whatever differences may be perceived inside the organization. As a minimum, it will confirm that 'means' have indeed become 'ends'.

The initiatives we have studied are all two or more years old, so it is unclear whether the time-lag effect has passed. However, we are satisfied that we have been able to assess accurately both the changes and the potential for change which each initiative has enabled so far in the organizations we studied.

Methodology

We recognize that there are some methodological problems in writing about change as it happens. First, many pressures are applied at the same time. For example, a manager may be faced simultaneously with a set of performance targets which are left over from a previous initiative while also facing a target of profitability in a competitive environment. Hence she might be competitive on price, tested against outside competition but still have to meet a target of a reduction in running costs. To isolate the effect of one target on behaviour is therefore a matter of judgement.

Secondly, there may be big differences between the rhetoric involved in the introduction of an initiative and the interpretation of its reality by managers. For example, the rhetoric might be about 'the freedom to manage', 'tough attitudes' and so on. The managers may see only the control by someone else of recruitment, pay scales, grades and the details of running costs. These constraints may be real or imagined. Interviews can only reveal perceptions.

The other problem with interviewing managers who are under pressure is that they may not be able to see the big picture. Recent events and pressure may obscure the underlying structural changes. Structural changes such as the introduction of competition may produce adjustments to cost, to quality, to the size and nature of the workforce and many other elements of the organization. An individual manager may be responsible for one element which then dominates his or her perception. We are confident that we have conducted a large enough number of interviews to have gained a significant selection of partial perspectives.

A further problem is that even if managers and observers produce a convincing analysis they may still not know how to act. The latter parts of this book are prescriptive, setting out how we think managers should behave to produce good services which respond to their users' needs and preferences. The prescriptions cannot be derived directly from the research: they are also based on an understanding of management practice in many sectors.

Our sources of information are varied. Some of the evidence in the book is derived from secondary sources and from informal contact with managers in a variety of public services. Other evidence comes from a series of interviews with a range of managers and workers in nine organizations undergoing managerial changes. These include five of the first Executive Agencies established under the Next Steps Initiative (Efficiency Unit, 1988). These were the Warren Spring Laboratory, Her Majesty's Stationery Office, the National Weights and Measures Laboratory, Companies House and the Vehicle Inspectorate. Interviews were also conducted in the Department of Social Security which went through a process of managerial decentralization before it was split into a Department and a group of Executive Agencies in April 1991.

The other organizations provide a range of experiences: Kent Education Authority devolved responsibility to schools in anticipation of the Education Reform Act and gives an opportunity to see the impact of both decentralization and competition among schools. An example of decentralization without competition is given by Northamptonshire Police. This is a case of a manager, the Chief Constable, trying to find mechanisms other than competition to improve management accountability and produce a more responsive service.

The final detailed example is London Buses Ltd (LBL). Competition is apparent here, both between buses and other means of transport and direct competition for tendered routes. The organization has been split into a series of independent companies and operational management has been further devolved to individual garages. It might be thought that LBL is no longer a 'real' public sector organization since it is organized along business lines and is preparing for privatization. It is, however, still publicly owned and subject to both a degree of social obligation and public accountability.

The sample of organizations provides a range of types of 'market' environment and approaches to managerial initiatives. HMSO has many activities which are purely commercial and for which they have to compete with private companies. London Buses Ltd are in competition but still have a high degree of regulation and control from the government and through London Regional Transport. The Police Force and the Department of Social Security are examples of attempts to devolve managerial responsibility even without the introduction of competition.

Therefore our first step, in Chapter 2, is to dissect the changes and try to organize them into some kind of competitive spectrum. This chapter introduces the organizations we have studied in detail and considers, for each of them, whether they are truly in a competitive environment, or whether they are suffering from 'market rhetoric'. Other managers may use this framework to decide where, if at all, their own organization fits on a competitive spectrum.

One consequence of adopting the 'bureaucratic equivalent of "market sentiment" is that business language can come to be used indiscriminately, without taking into consideration the underlying realities of the relationship between the organization and its stakeholders. This rhetorical difficulty exacerbates an existing conundrum in the public sector, namely what should be the relationship between the organization and its users? For example, does the prison service provide custodial care or custodial care and rehabilitation? For many years, managers did not confront such important fundamental questions about their work because the public sector was somehow supposed to satisfy a huge range of stakeholders and to attempt to be something to everybody. One useful impact of initiatives designed to make the public sector more business-like was that ideas of strategic planning started to be contemplated seriously from around 1986. For example, the Civil Service College launched a Strategic Planning course for the first time in 1988. Previously, strategy had been felt the domain of ministers and Parliament, while public sector officials merely implemented policy. The strength of strategic planning is that it encourages such fundamental questions to be asked.

Assuming that public sector managers feel empowered to 'go public' about their *raison d'être*, ideas of competition can provide a fairly simple and energizing form of rallying cry in the attempt to improve efficiency. However, what then tends to happen is that some managers take ideas of competition beyond acceptable bounds. For example, Executive Agencies are not allowed to compete with private sector companies: if the service can be provided by the private sector, then let it do so. Managers then complain that they are being asked to compete with one hand tied behind their backs. In fact, they are often not being asked to 'compete' at all, just to become more efficient and outcome-focused. On the other hand, entrepreneurship can go beyond acceptable limits: while wishing our public sector to become more proactive, we are still not prepared to accept mistakes. The innovative interest rate swaps by the London Borough of Hammersmith and Fulham are just one example of entrepreneurship taken a step too far, straight into the Courts. The rhetoric can therefore intrude and confuse and, despite early successes, can then further sour and disenchant employees. Chapter 3 therefore suggests that managers analyse their own organizations, so that the appropriate language and actions follow from the reality of the situation in which the organization finds itself. Should a public sector organization truly find itself facing competition, then its managers need to consider how they will compete.

Often a simple choice of price competition is made. However, there are other options and this chapter allows the manager to explore these and consider their relevance.

Should competition not prove to be an appropriate metaphor, are there other options open to managers so that they can encourage the energy necessary to make changes happen? It seems to us that there are at least two. The first, explored in Chapter 4, is decentralization. It has been suggested for many years that fewer management layers and smaller, self-contained organizations encourage managers to behave differently. While Henry Mintzberg (1983) is probably the most well-known recent international writer on this subject, questions about motivation at work have been pursued by psychologists and sociologists since the 1920s. Anthony Jay (1972) explored his experiences at the British Broadcasting Corporation and concluded that smaller work units encourage greater ownership of the outputs and that shared responsibility for task achievement encourages both commitment and creativity. This work provided further empirical evidence of the theories of earlier writers and finds echoes in later writers, such as Kennedy and Deal (1982), Handy (1989) and Hampden-Turner (1990), who write about the importance of internal cohesion or corporate culture in determining the spirit and success of organizations.

In Chapter 4 we assess the extent to which decentralization is really happening in the organizations we studied and therefore the extent to which it can be used to increase the motivation and commitment of the people who work inside them. This energy can produce new ways of working.

One could argue that the importance of small autonomous work units, limited layers of management (current theory suggests four) and delegation in encouraging motivation far precedes the work of American theorists in the 1920s, or even philosophers of the eighteenth century.

A quotation from Exodus 18, 21–22 makes it clear that these issues have been recognized for a long time.

> Moreover, thou shalt provide out of all the people able men such as fear God, men of truth, hating covetousness; and place such over them, to be rulers of thousands, and rulers of hundreds, rulers of fifties, and rulers of tens:
> And let them judge the people at all seasons; and it shall be, that every great matter they shall bring unto thee, but every small matter they shall judge; so shall it be easier for thyself, and they shall bear the burden with thee.

We suggest that the second method for releasing energy is actually a return to a core value held by public sector managers for generations, that of providing public service. It is clear that policies pursued since 1979 have led many public sector managers to believe that cost cutting and cutting the numbers employed in the public sector far outweighed any other considerations. However, becoming more business-like has, since the late 1980s, come to mean also improving the service to users. There has been a move to call users or clients, 'customers', paralleling a greater customer-focus in the private sector. However, the rhetorical overlay of calling 'users', 'customers', can reinstate earlier difficulties or create new ones. For example, does being a customer imply some level of choice? If you lock me up in prison, how am I being served? Or are customers distinct from users? Assuming that earlier chapters have helped managers to answer some of these questions and assuming that one of the fundamental purposes of any organization is to serve its users to the limit of its capacity, Chapter 5 is about the most important success measure, the impact of these changes upon recipients of the service. Public sector managers from Executive Agencies, from the Police, from Education and from Transport have shared with us their views about the changes and the differences these have made to their work practices and attitudes. Some of the organizations have also looked at the impact of the changes upon their users and where we have their permission to share this, we do so. Unfortunately, the penalty for experimentation or 'failure' is still considered too high by some and where the outcome is not straightforward improvement, we have sometimes been asked to keep the outcome confidential. It seems that we must be much more tolerant of 'failure' if we are to encourage the new proactive culture that so many senior public sector managers and Ministers and Councillors seem to desire. It is hard to see how one can espouse a core value like 'A bias for action' if every action needs to be considered by committee and signed in triplicate before it can be made safe enough to implement.

Chapter 6 explores the elements of good service delivery. Whether we call the people whom we serve customers, users or clients seems largely immaterial, except to the extent again that the rhetoric can inspire. What is more important is the detailed managerial activity necessary to design and deliver good service.

This further implies different ways of working for many managers. Bureaucracy is an appropriate form of working for processing large amounts of routine work in a systematic manner. It is less appropriate for encouraging creativity or ownership of the decisions taken to the extent that individuals have a personal commitment to their implementation. We explore what some of the new values espoused by public sector organizations actually mean in terms of the behaviours required from managers.

Chapter 7 examines the problems of implementing change. It seems that there are generic lessons which can be learned from such a diversity of public sector organizations. Other public sector managers can therefore avoid some of the painful progression up the learning curve of change which these organizations have already travelled. Moreover, it is clear from our analysis that, as ever, across-the-board solutions cannot solve specific problems. In considering what aspects might improve the effectiveness of the change process in the public sector organizations we have studied, we hope to provide insights for other managers across the public sector.

2 Competitive environment

'We feel asked to operate as a business, but hampered by the level of control still exercised by the Government. We will be allowed to compete for the business, but are constrained by not being allowed to advertise our service.'
(Interview with a manager in an Executive Agency)

In this chapter we look at the likely effect on managerial behaviour of implementing initiatives in the public sector which seem to introduce elements of market relationships. The qualifying 'seem to' is important. Market or competitive rhetoric is frequently used even in cases where the organizations either do not compete at all, or only at the margin of their activities. Therefore we also look more closely at the actual changes which have been made and propose a taxonomy of types of markets. Our sample of organizations covers the whole spectrum.

Most of the reforms which purport to introduce competition stop short of establishing free, competitive markets. We would define a free market as having at least the following features:

1   Customers would be able to make a choice, both of the service to be purchased and of the provider.
2   Providers would be allowed to attract customers, by producing what customers want and by adjusting price and quality.
3   There would be enough information on price, quality and availability to enable the market to operate.
4   There would be a sufficiently large number of purchasers and providers for both sides to be able to choose, and for no individual purchaser or provider to be able to determine the price. This may imply that there is free entry into the market and the possibility of suppliers ceasing to supply and exiting from the market.

Not all of these conditions are met in all of the reforms which the government has introduced. At its minimum level, a market reform simply divides the organization into two parts, which are labelled the 'purchaser' and the 'provider'. If nothing else changes, such a reform may have little impact. Such an outcome could happen in the NHS in an area which has one District Health Authority (DHA) and one District General Hospital. The hospital management and staff become the providers and the people remaining in the DHA become purchasers. If there is no other accessible hospital and there are no GP fundholders, no great impact would be expected on managerial behaviour: there is no competition; patients have no choice of where to go; the providers have no incentives to do better; nobody else is able to enter the market.

We might say the same about some of the changes in the Civil Service which divide a Department into one or more Executive Agencies and a rump Department which provides policy advice and purchases services from the Agency. Here, the Agency is not allowed to attract customers and sell its services other than to the Department. 'Customers' still have no choice. Instead of there being a combined 'buyer' and 'seller', the department is now divided into a monopoly provider and a monopsony (or single) purchaser.

Evidence given to the Treasury and Civil Service Select Committee on 17 June 1991 by Michael Bichard, the Chief Executive of the new Benefits Agency, gives one example of how this might work. Nick Montagu, his accompanying Civil Servant (the Personnel and Finance Officer of the Department of Social Security) explained that HQ staff had been reduced from 4000 to 1200, thus exceeding the target of a 25% headquarters staff reduction recommended in the Efficiency Unit report of May 1991 (Making the Most of Next Steps, Efficiency Unit, HMSO). Further questioning from John Garrett MP revealed that no one had lost their job: all had been transferred to one of the four Agencies set up by the Department and in some cases, staff had not even moved offices.

Social Services departments are also dividing themselves into purchasers and providers. The Griffiths report (1988) suggested that these two functions should be separated, partly to clarify the services which are provided and their cost, partly to reduce the bias towards existing service providers, and partly to enable new entrants to the market. Whether this reform generates a free market as defined above depends on how the 'market' develops. Service users are still dependent on the department to gain access to services which are funded by them. In this sense the first condition, choice for customers, does not apply. If there are no alternative suppliers, the market again consists only of a monopoly provider and a monopsony purchaser.

We might call this minimum level of reform 'playing at shops' (Figure 2.1). The only change from the previous arrangement is that the organizations are divided into two parts, a buyer and a seller.

A variant on this is a position in which a monopoly is sustained, but there are many buyers of the service (Figure 2.2).

Stage two introduces competition between providers, either within the

Figure 2.1   Monopoly/monopsony ('playing at shops')

public sector, or between public and private providers. Here there is still a single purchaser, but the purchaser is able to organize competition among providers. For example, a local authority is responsible for street cleaning and refuse collection from houses in its area. Authorities are now compelled to organize periodic competitions for the contract to provide these services.

In community care there are likely to be a number of providers of certain services in a local authority area. While the local authority is the only channel through which government funds flow, services could be provided by other public agencies and by the private and voluntary sectors. We could call this situation a monopsony/competitive market (Figure 2.3).

A still more competitive market is established if there is more than one purchaser, and provider units are able to seek out 'customers'. For example, in urban areas community care follows this pattern: providers are able to cross local authority boundaries and provide services to more than one purchaser.

In the NHS a DHA may be the only 'purchaser' operating in an area but may choose to use its funds to purchase services from a variety of hospitals and other providers. Meanwhile, hospitals are also able to enter contracts with other, accessible authorities or GP fundholders. We might call this situation a competitive internal market (Figure 2.4).

Once alternative suppliers, outside the public sector, are introduced, as they are in the NHS reforms, the market ceases to be internal and becomes

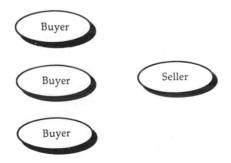

Figure 2.2   Monopoly/more than one purchaser

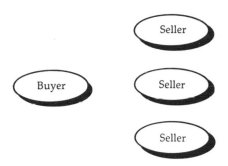

Figure 2.3 Monopsony/more than one provider

an open market. Even without individual consumer choice of supplier, this opening of the market subjects the internal suppliers to a different pressure.

To satisfy condition four, that there should be a large number of purchasers and providers operating competitively, there would need to be greater freedom than is implied by this internal market. Providers would need to be able to supply to a greater variety of purchasers and be able to seek them out. Without this condition, the providers are subject to control by the purchasers who are able to collude with each other. Indeed as the NHS reforms were implemented there were many cases of formal and informal purchaser consortia being formed to increase purchasing power, while the providers have limited scope to sell elsewhere.

Where do the customers fit?

So far we have discussed market forms without examining the position of the user of the services. It is possible to exclude consumer choice from

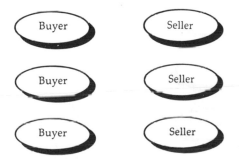

Figure 2.4 Competitive internal market

administratively constructed markets: the local authority might organize a competition among contractors, but the individual citizen may still have no option but to accept the chosen contractor. Individual patients are still dependent on a referral to hospital, although they may be able to influence the choice of provider.

For the managers, the position of the consumer is crucial: if consumers have choice, their selling efforts should be directed towards the individuals, whereas if all 'sales' are made through an intermediary, the sales effort has to be made towards the purchasers. On the other hand, if service users have a choice of 'purchaser', then the purchasers have to engage in marketing and selling to attract users. In the case of fundholder GPs, for example, patients have a degree of choice about which purchaser to use.

If we introduce service users to the market, there is the possibility of condition one, consumer choice, being satisfied. We might call this situation a competitive market with consumer choice. It is illustrated in Figure 2.5.

However, there is still a crucial difference between this situation and a 'real' market. In all the cases of reformed markets, the amount of funding is still determined by government, whether central or local. In 'real' markets, the amount of cash is determined by a series of choices by individuals about how to spend their own income. An analysis of the new markets without recognizing this would be an illusion: we should not expect managers to adopt competitive behaviour by influencing consumers and purchasers without having regard to the ultimate source of funds. We could describe this form of market as a competitive market with politics (Figure 2.6).

The market reforms have been designed to achieve changes in managerial behaviour. Competition is expected to generate an impetus among providers for survival and/or growth which should result in a

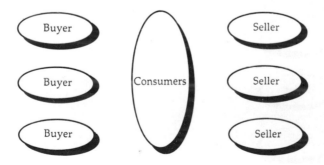

Figure 2.5   Competitive market with limited consumer choice

concern for price and therefore cost. If purchasers are keen to get the best value for money they will organize the purchasing process so that prices are held down. It may also be the case that purchasers will be able to act on behalf of the users to improve quality, if sufficient funds are available and if the right mechanisms are created.

To evaluate the reforms the key question to ask is how do the reforms affect managers, whether purchasers or providers? In this chapter we look at the structural changes from both points of view as well as from the perspective of the service users. In the next chapter we look at how managers have used the structural changes to provide more efficient and effective services.

The provider's point of view

One major purpose of introducing market mechanisms and competition is to have some impact on the people providing public services. The impact could be achieved through positive or negative incentives: success might produce rewards of cash or greater satisfaction; failure might result in shrinkage or closure. To make these incentives work they must have an impact on workers and managers. In turn, they must be able to take action to enable them to be competitive.

We now consider the competitive position of each of the organizations according to the definitions of market types given above (see Figure 2.7 on page 32).

The National Weights and Measures Laboratory (NWML) became an Executive Agency on 18 April 1989 and was the most unusual of the early Agencies. It is very small (50 staff in one building on a site in Teddington, Middlesex) and 75% of its work is policy work funded under the Department's Vote, drafting new regulations, representing its parent

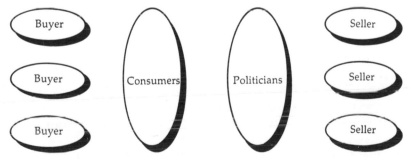

Figure 2.6 Competitive market with consumer choice but still some political control

Department, the Department of Trade and Industry, in Brussels and so on. (The original idea of the Executive Agency initiative was that it should apply to organizations delivering services, not undertaking policy advice work.) The remaining 25% of its activities is fee earning work. NWML is responsible for the administration of weights and measures legislation, in particular the regulation and certification of equipment in use for trade. This includes work on European harmonization, commercially confidential testing work for manufacturers and the Trial of the Pyx (trial plates presented annually at the Trial to ensure that coinage issued by the Royal Mint is within legal specifications).

NWML actually faces no competition for the majority of its work of policy formulation. The former Chief Executive, Dr Peter Clapham, felt that no good purpose would be served by opening up this area of work to market forces. He felt that quality and efficiency would actually suffer under any alternative system one might devise, such as creating an 'intelligent customer' to pre-select advice from competing sources. NWML also retains a monopoly in providing statutory certification services for manufacturers. What it has sought to do is to encourage competition in the supply chain towards gaining a certificate, through encouraging manufacturers to use private sector test houses and through holding training seminars for the employees of these private test houses, so that they can offer better and more competitive services. It also tries to work with manufacturers during the development of new equipment (such as petrol pumps) so that any problems can be spotted and dealt with early, well before production starts. NWML expects to face increased competition from European test houses from 1992.

In NWML one sees the almost classic clash between ideals of a free market place and those of regulation with a minimum burden for the taxpayer. A private sector monopoly might well wish to unburden itself from the majority of the testing work, but still to charge the maximum price possible for issuing the all-important certificate. It would probably also seek to grow, both in influence and in profits. Indeed, Dr Clapham explained that some European Community members with semi-privatized type approval agencies were arguing in Brussels for more legal controls, which would incidentally increase their levels of business. The UK, on the contrary, was arguing for a policy of deregulation, to reduce the burden on business, because as part of the Department of Trade and Industry, their primary concern is not profit, but the needs of the business community.

The actual strategy pursued, therefore, was one of encouraging and enabling increasing degrees of self-certification by manufacturers, of decreasing its level of influence as much as possible, of cutting costs and keeping prices to customers as low as possible and of trying to adopt a more customer-friendly rather than policing approach towards its service users. NWML continues to seek non-statutory work to help defray overheads on its expensive equipment, but has no desire to grow and does not advertise in case it cannot cope with any demand thus stimulated.

On our competitive spectrum, it is involved in little more than 'playing at shops' for the majority of its work in policy advice: it has been separated to a degree from the parent Department, but is still a monopoly supplier facing a monopsony purchaser. The situation is a little different so far as its type certification approval work is concerned: here there is some competition along the supply chain, which we might typify as a competitive market with consumer choice, (position 4 on the spectrum), in that manufacturers are actually encouraged by NWML to choose among testing agencies, of which it is one. However, when it comes to issuing the type approval certificate, we are back to playing at shops: the customer has only one choice, NWML. Assuming that its overall approach will be shaped by the market location of most of its work, NWML can be placed at position 1 of the competitive spectrum.

Our next organization, Her Majesty's Stationery Office (HMSO), provides a contrast. It is a mature business, founded in 1786, in a mature industry, that of printing, publishing and the supply of office requisites. It is a separate Government Department, headquartered in Norwich, a Trading Fund (since 1980) and on 14 December 1988 also became an Executive Agency. One would expect Agency status to have least impact on this organization, because Trading Fund status means that they were already free of Government rules on gross running cost control (control over gross expenditure, regardless of income generated) or annuality (the requirement to balance the books within every year). Other Government Departments were freed in 1982 from the requirement to buy all stationery and printing through HMSO. It does retain a monopoly on Parliamentary printing, a £28 million business in 1988 on a total turnover of about £330 million. It sees itself in a competitive environment, as this extract from a 1989 internal memo from the Chief Executive, Dr Paul Freeman (a Civil Servant), makes clear: '... the world does not owe us a living. We can only survive for as long as the value added by our involvement outweighs any additional cost.'

HMSO has a turnover of about £330 million and reduced its staff numbers from 6300 in 1980 to 3200 in 1989. There are four product divisions, Supply, Print Procurement, Publications and Production, but there are Account Executives so that each large customer has one contact to coordinate their requirements. There is internal trade between the Divisions, e.g. Print Procurement buys some paper from Supply Division, but transfer prices are fixed so that there is no cross-subsidization.

Supply Division is the largest business and supplies a variety of office needs, from toilet paper to desk top computers. It buys from manufacturers and suppliers at large discounts for bulk purchases and then passes the goods on to customers. Three-quarters of turnover comes from central Government customers, the other 25% from other public sector bodies like local authorities. Print Procurement Division is the largest print buyer in the UK. Again its role is to buy more cheaply than individual customers could (although here the cheapness is achieved through expertise in choosing the most appropriate printer and through competition between printers) and then to pass some of these savings on. Most of the work (80%) is contracted out and there are 1200 approved printers on the list. Again, 80% of work in this market is for central Government, with the remainder being for other public sector bodies such as Health Authorities. It prints a range of products from passports to doctors' prescription forms. Publications Division produces about 9000 new titles a year and is one of the world's largest publishers. It publishes Government Acts, *Hansard*, the Highway Code and more general paperback titles. It has a huge storage warehouse at Nine Elms in London: account holders can order by post but HMSO also has six bookshops around the UK. The fourth Division is that of Production, which has five printing works and seven reprographic units. This Division prints mainly Parliamentary, security and classified work. Parliamentary work is not done on a repayment basis, unlike other work, but is funded through the Vote and HMSO retains a virtual monopoly on this work. A little overnight printing is contracted out but, for example, the Lords' *Hansard* has been brought in house because competition showed HMSO was cheaper and in-house facilities have therefore been modernized, upgraded and expanded to keep pace with demand.

We said above that HMSO is a Trading Fund. This means that in 1980 it was valued and a corresponding amount was deemed to have been loaned to it from the National Loans Fund at a fixed rate of interest. This has to be repaid by 1995. Additional loans may be taken from the National Loans Fund, e.g. to meet in-year cash fluctuations (customers who are Government Departments funded annually from the Vote, have to spend all their allocations in-year, which can cause HMSO some end-year difficulties).

HMSO has come under increasing competitive pressure over recent years. There was a fair amount of inertia in the system when Government Departments were first untied from HMSO supply in 1982. However, increasing market fragmentation, through initiatives like the restructuring of Government services into Executive Agencies, has meant that customers are more willing to ask for alternative tenders, in order to obtain tailor-made services which better suit their needs. Some suppliers of office stationery and equipment are also willing to bypass HMSO and supply customers direct when asked. As a public sector body, HMSO does not take direct retaliatory action, such as not using these suppliers any more, although they may be featured less prominently in the HMSO catalogue.

The market is moving towards smaller bespoke orders and a quicker response time, particularly on the stationery side. This means that HMSO has lost work to some more proactive competitors who also offer an across-the-range service. These competitors have won work, for example, by offering small monthly orders delivered to the desk, with a 24-hour turnaround on orders. This move away from HMSO bulk orders being delivered direct to the customer from the original supplier has implications for HMSO warehousing size and location, as more customers ask for retail, just-in-time delivery. However, this should not be over-emphasized. In 1990, 70% of business came from 13 customers, with 60% from the top three customer Government Departments. This concentration brings its own problems. A small number of powerful buyers puts these buyers in a strong bargaining position and HMSO is increasingly pressed to offer larger discounts. Some large Departments are employing professional purchasing advisers and setting up their own direct procurement arrangements on the grounds that their purchasing muscle is at least equal to HMSO's.

The market is therefore pushing HMSO strategy in two directions. With large customers threatening to go independent unless lower prices are forthcoming, HMSO has to try to cut costs as the only way to retain profitability. Customers are increasingly unconvinced by talk of long-term value for money and prefer to think in terms of a quick bargain. Biros are a good example. The HMSO Laboratory conducts tests to make sure that they choose suppliers who offer not the cheapest, but the longest-running biro. Customers, however, say that as most biros are lost long before they run out, the cheapest will do. As some customers now say that they can obtain just as low prices direct, the second change HMSO is attempting is to offer more added value. They emphasize the value of the technical advice their staff give, they offer training in desk-top publishing and they offer printing, storage and distribution as a package. There is increasing emphasis on service quality through tailoring services to individual requirements.

HMSO seems to fall at the other end of our competitive spectrum from the National Weights and Measures Laboratory. It is at position 6, a competitive market with politics. HMSO have a single purchaser (the Government) for Parliamentary printing; they also have users or customers. There is more than one provider than HMSO, i.e. all their competitors. There is a profit motive, because as a Trading Fund, HMSO can retain some profit for investment. So where do the politics come in? It is not true to say, in this case, that Government determines the level of funding centrally. Legislation precludes them from supplying the private sector, while they are at the same time supposed to tolerate and respond to competition from the private sector. They retain core Civil Service values like equity, i.e. equal access to service: this stops them discarding unprofitable business (the nearest they come to this is to attempt to discourage some smaller orders through price) and so prevents a purely commercial outlook.

The exception to this classification is in HMSO's monopoly in Parliamentary printing. This probably falls at position 3 in the spectrum, because although there is one supplier facing one purchaser (our definition of playing at shops), in fact the purchaser keeps an eye on the alternatives by periodically checking HMSO's prices against the competition. This therefore looks like a monopsony facing a competitive market. Or as a HMSO manager describes it: 'I saw HMSO as a large lumbering dinosaur. Now I see them as lots of little dinosaurs, some of them trying to move quite fast, in fact, trying to evolve.'

Our third example is the Vehicle Inspectorate (VI), a monopoly and a regulatory authority, which became the first Executive Agency on 1 August 1988. Its task is to ensure the roadworthiness of vehicles. It does this in a number of ways. About 70% of staff are involved in the initial and then annual testing of all Heavy Goods' Vehicles (HGVs) and Public Service Vehicles (PSVs). HGVs are tested at Vehicle Inspectorate's own testing stations and PSVs at the same stations or at approved operators' premises. Vehicle Inspectorate also inspects workshops authorized to fit and calibrate tachographs.

In addition, it operates the MOT scheme for private cars. Fourteen per cent of staff are involved in authorizing all MOT testing stations (there are nearly 18 000 of these), training and approving nominated testers, making regular and unannounced inspections of MOT stations and issuing MOT Certificate pads for testers. Eight per cent of staff work on assessing and reporting on HGV and PSV operators' maintenance arrangements and fleet condition, through programmed and surprise checks. Other work involves random roadside checks to test the roadworthiness of HGVs, PSVs and Light Goods Vehicles including cars and motorbikes (it can prohibit the use of defective vehicles) and also investigation of road accidents where poor vehicle condition may have been a contributory factor.

It was decided not to privatize Vehicle Inspectorate following a review in 1983, but it was subsequently reorganized into a separate business unit within the Department of Transport. It was given exemption from gross running cost control on 1 April 1988 (four months before it became an Agency), which means that it can spend more (or less) to react to changes in demand, as long as unit cost targets are met. It was therefore an 'Agency' before this status was formally conferred. Its senior managers face perhaps the most difficult management task of all the Executive Agencies we looked at, because of the wide geographic coverage of the business. It employs about 1600 staff and is headquartered in Bristol, but also has four regions with between one and four regional sub-offices in each, 53 District Offices and 91 HGV Testing Stations (of which 53 are also District Offices).

We see here again, as with the National Weights and Measures Laboratory, the tension between a commercial outlook and Government regulation. The Chief Executive, Mr Ron Oliver (a Civil Servant) says that the Inspectorate has two customers, road users and road safety. There is obviously a balancing act to be achieved between customer service and customer regulation. A crude example is given by the question, is it better to fail a lot of vehicles in order to improve road safety or to pass a lot of vehicles to improve customer satisfaction indices? At the most basic level, 'fining them with a smile' is a distinct possibility. The Agency initiative for Vehicle Inspectorate is certainly, at one level, about putting a more human face on a professional organization dedicated to road safety.

As a statutory regulatory authority, Vehicle Inspectorate has no competitors in its core business. The Inspectorate charges fees for all its statutory work which must no more than cover costs. Where new initiatives are extensions of its statutory duties, for example, out-of-hours testing is a more customer-friendly version of the core business, then again fees levied may only cover costs. However, where initiatives are an enhancement of customer service, but non-statutory, as for example, voluntary brake testing, commercial training, and publication and sale of Vehicle Inspectorate manuals, market prices may be charged. Market prices are obviously affected by the prices charged for competitive offerings, but because of the Inspectorate's unique status, they are also affected by two other things. One is the fact that the Inspectorate is a regulatory body. The reason for offering a new voluntary brake testing service is primarily one of road safety, because this is the major cause of vehicle test failure. However, if the vehicle proves defective during a voluntary test and the owner does not agree to have the fault remedied immediately, then the Inspectorate has the power to convert the test to a statutory one and insist that the vehicle is rectified straight away. Charging needs to be very competitive to overcome this disincentive. The other pressure on price is of course the Treasury, who have to approve profit levels on non-statutory work.

Again we see a business apparently willing to reduce its income in the absence of any competitive threat. The Inspectorate is considering a free or reduced retest fee where the cause of failure is minor and the vehicle can be adjusted for retest quickly. The Treasury is a surrogate market pressure demanding increasingly lower unit costs. This can have a beneficial impact on customers, not simply through the price mechanism. For example, in his written evidence to the Treasury and Civil Service Select Committee (Fifth

Report, 19 July 1989), Mr Ron Oliver said: 'In addition to efficiency savings made elsewhere, the Inspectorate needs to achieve a contribution in the region of £6–700 000 (2% of income: authors' calculation) by the end of 1990/1 from the successful launch of a range of business initiatives (i.e. additional activities) if its current cost efficiency target is to be met. These proposed business initiatives were retitled "customer service initiatives", as it quickly became clear to the organization that this more accurately reflected the overriding aim of providing new, improved and more responsive services to VIEA's customers.' Mr Oliver believes that acting as though there were competitors and not just at the margin, is necessary to engage managers' interest in enhancing basic service levels. In fact, the Inspectorate is not allowed to compete with the private sector for work, but has to stay close to its statutory duties and related activities. However, competition may really be increasing. From 18 March 1991 the HGV registration threshold was raised so that vehicles with a design gross weight of 3500 kg or less became classified as Light Goods Vehicles. Garages are now able to offer an MOT certificate in competition with Vehicle Inspectorate for this class of vehicle.

Vehicle Inspectorate is at position 1 on our spectrum, playing at shops. Although the individual users of the service pay for it, they have no choice of provider and the fee is set at a level, by Government, to recoup the costs of providing the service. The Government has therefore decided what the burden of regulation should be and has separated out from itself the Agency to enforce this regulation. The small amount of non-statutory work is only there to help Vehicle Inspectorate meet its efficiency targets at the margin.

Our fourth example is another laboratory. Warren Spring Laboratory (WSL) provides research and technical services on environmental technology and pollution problems. Its Chief Executive, Dr John Reay (previously a Civil Servant) heads a workforce of just over 300, all located at Stevenage in Hertfordshire, apart from four people in a small laboratory in East Kilbride. Nearly 70% of staff are scientists or technicians. Warren Spring does about £10 million worth of business a year, about 75% for the public sector, 14% for jointly funded public and private sector projects and 11% directly for industry.

Warren Spring's parent Department is the Department of Trade and Industry. A Ministerial review of Research Establishments in 1989 agreed that Warren Spring should run down (to nil by 1992/3) the 23% of industrially relevant work wholly funded by Department of Trade and Industry Divisions acting as a proxy for industry (an extreme example of playing at shops which Ministers decided to discontinue). At the same time it was agreed that it should limit to 10% each the two areas of jointly funded work and work for the private sector alone. Warren Spring has also moved to a clearer customer/contractor relationship with the Department of Trade and Industry, i.e. a move to repayment terms (as it has had for years for work undertaken for other Government Departments). Furthermore, all Government customers are encouraged to go to tender for commissioned work. Warren Spring has to cover its costs, although it is allowed a small surcharge to go towards funding strategic research, which will grow from about 2 to about 10% of income. They have 15 major long-term customers, all Government Departments, six of them customer Divisions within the Department of Trade and Industry. Services are provided on different contractual terms for different customers, e.g. 20% of its resources are paid for by the Department of the Environment on the basis of an annual letter.

Competition is increasing now that Warren Spring has moved to repayment contracts and there is open tender for Department of Trade and Industry work. Many of its potential collaborators and subcontractors are also its competitors. The vast majority are public sector bodies: the Health and Safety Executive, the Pollution Inspectorate of the Department of the Environment, Harwell, Universities, environmental research associations and local authorities, as well as engineering consultants. Warren Spring is pursuing the by-now familiar strategy of cost cutting, both in response to customers going to open tender for work and in response to the Treasury, who are placing continuing emphasis on cost savings. Again we see an Agency opened up to competition, but being restricted in its competitive strategy: Warren Spring may only seek to expand its customer base in the public sector. It is doing this (to local authority or European work) in order to spread overheads more widely and thus reduce unit costs.

Dr Reay is keen on competition as a spur to efficiency. However, their relationship with their customers is not entirely arms' length. Major capital investment is still funded out of Department of Trade and Industry Vote money. Dr Reay also hopes that open tendering procedures will take the long-term view: price alone should not be the deciding factor, but also the Government's interest in retaining a source of expertise. Warren Spring is cheaper than most of its private sector competitors, but its price competitiveness is not so clear cut compared to other public sector bodies.

Warren Spring is at point 4 on the competitive spectrum, facing a competitive internal market. It is not the only provider and also faces more than one purchaser. Its 10% of private sector work, where users have a direct choice about which provider to choose, would be placed at position 5 on the spectrum, i.e. a competitive market with consumer choice. However, again, we believe that the locus of its major work will determine its outlook and organizational culture: hence we place it at position 4.

The last Executive Agency we looked at is Companies House. Companies House is a monopoly. Underpinned by legislation, it is required to register new companies and information about companies, process information on companies moving into liquidation and in the course of dissolution, strike companies off the register as necessary, ensure that companies comply with their obligations in terms of registering information and store this information and make it available to the public. The phrase 'underpinned by legislation' is important, because there is, for example, no specific requirement in the legislation for the Chief Executive to chase companies who do not submit accounts and returns. Nonetheless, this is obviously an important task because it seeks to ensure both conformity with the spirit of the law and that the database is broad enough to offer a good service to those wishing to investigate company accounts. Companies House employs 1100 people in Cardiff, London and Edinburgh and became an Executive Agency on 3 October 1988 under Mr Stephen Curtis (a Civil Servant) as Chief Executive. The current Chief Executive is Mr David Durham.

Companies House has about one million companies on its records, about 800 000 of which are 'live'. Customers ask for four million over-the-counter and about 55 000 postal searches a year. They have 400 regular over-the-counter customers in London and 40 in Cardiff. These regular users are mostly Agents like Jordans or Dunn & Bradstreet, carrying out searches on behalf of clients. The top 20 Agents request about 80% of the searches. Companies House has about 500 Account Holder customers, who have access to a postal and a fax search service. Fee income in 1988/9 was about £33 million.

Like many of the Agencies, Companies House was becoming more efficient before it became an Agency. This is similar to John Kay's findings on privatization, i.e. that it is the most efficient which are privatized, not the privatized which become most efficient. For example, compliance (the percentage of live companies which have submitted their latest returns and accounts) was only 40% in 1984, compared to 80% in 1988, the year they became an Agency. Keeping the records up to date is an enormous exercise: they receive about 14 000 documents every day from companies.

Although Companies House has become much more efficient and has also made its service delivery more local, through using the Department of Trade and Industry regional office network and through offering postal and fax services, many customers never have direct contact with Companies House at all. This is partly because of its former poor record on service delivery. Companies did not have the time to waste, sending employees to London or Cardiff to carry out a slow search process. Instead, intermediary Agents entered the market, who would carry out searches on customers' behalf. Some of these simply carry out the searches and report the raw data to customers: others, like Dunn & Bradstreet, also analyse the data to give, for example, credit ratings on the companies under review. These agents actually make Companies House's task easier, because they batch sort requests and also order in bulk. However, there is no doubt that managers in the Executive Agency resent the no-value-added interlopers and hope to see their market share diminish. Companies House has, however, to overcome many years conditioning on the part of their customers. Market research shows that its customers, when comparing Companies House and these Agents, generally favour the Agents, although the Executive Agency is trying hard to alter these perceptions.

Like the other Agencies, Companies House is pursuing a cost-cutting strategy. They are also trying to grow their market but intend to meet increased demand through greater productivity rather than increased resources. Again like others, they are trying to raise extra income by offering new, customer-focused services, which brought in about £1 million additional income in 1988/9. These new services look at market, rather than cost recovery, pricing, but are strictly limited to those which complement its legislative duties. It will not diversify away from its core business and is precluded from competing with the private sector, e.g. by adding value through analysing company information.

Companies House is at position 1 on the spectrum as far as its company registration activity is concerned. The Government requires companies to register information and has set up an Agency at arm's length to carry out this work. There is only one purchaser, the Government, and only one provider, Companies House Executive Agency. It is more difficult to be categoric about its supply of company information. To a certain extent, there is at least the appearance of being more than one provider, because of the intermediary agencies which have set up. Users, or direct consumers, also enter the picture as companies buy the information from Companies House, or indirectly through an agency. While this does not alter the fundamental market truth, which is that Companies House is a monopoly, the appearance of competition may help its managers to become more committed to increasing their efficiency. Thus while our analysis might place them in the playing at shops category, we believe that their managers (and indeed their customers) may perceive themselves to be at position 5, a competitive market with consumer choice.

We also looked at the four other public sector organizations which were not Executive Agencies, although one of them has subsequently become an Agency. The Department of Social Security (now split into the Department and four Agencies including the Benefits Agency) is a huge national organization designed to deliver Social Security benefits through a national organization which includes a network of over 800 local offices serving every community in Great Britain. Claims for benefit are received and dealt with either in the local office, or at centralized offices in

Newcastle, Washington or Blackpool. At the time of the study each local office was run by a Local Office Manager.

Although there was a drive in the Civil Service generally towards cost effectiveness, especially following the financial management initiative (FMI), change in this department also resulted from two specific reports. One was on the flow of work between local offices and regional offices and between regional offices and headquarters. This report, known as the 'traffic study', written in 1981, recommended that more work should be contained within the local offices. The second report, by Price Waterhouse Associates in 1982, recommended the introduction of a new budgetary control system for administrative expenditure. These reports formed the basis of the department's response to the FMI. Decentralization to local office managers was an important element of the response.

Social security payments are set by statute and rules of eligibility which leaves very little scope for managerial discretion. A small amount of discretion is allowed to Social Fund Officers who have to make choices according to the budgetary position. Therefore on the competitive spectrum it should be placed at position 1: it is a monopoly supplier with a monopsony purchaser. The claimants (now called customers) are not the *purchasers* of the service, the Government is. While there is a possibility of competition from, say, Post Office Counters, there is currently no alternative distributor of benefits.

Our seventh example is Northamptonshire Police. This police force is divided into two geographical divisions, each containing three subdivisions. An average subdivision is policed by around 200 officers. Each subdivision is commanded by a Superintendent with a Chief Inspector as his/her deputy. There is also a civilian Chief Administration Officer. Police forces are roughly evenly financed by the county councils and Home Office, so in effect they compete for resources but not against each other in their area of primary concern, that of law enforcement.

Instead of separating purchasers from providers, the force has attempted to improve management through a process of decentralization. The motivation for decentralizing the force came from Maurice Buck, the Chief Constable from 1982 to 1986. He was committed to 'policing by objectives' (PBO) which had been promoted by the Police Staff College at Bramshill. The version of PBO which Buck adopted stipulated that the Chief Constable sets the policy framework expressed in goal statements. Objectives are then set at divisional level with reference to the goal statements and individual Inspectors, at subdivisional level, have to draw up action plans for achieving the objectives. This process implies accountability for actions at both subdivisional level and within individual stations.

We place Northamptonshire police at position 2 on the spectrum because in the county at least, they are the monopoly law enforcement supplier. Any competitor is extremely marginal, such as private security firms guarding factory premises. They are attempting to manage as if they have more than one purchaser and are making attempts to treat the public as if they were their customers, as we shall see in Chapter 5.

Our eighth example is Kent Local Education Authority (LEA). Schools in Kent are divided into six geographical areas. Each area has its own Area Education Officer, responsible for providing the services of the LEA to the schools. At the time of the research, a pilot scheme of schools in Kent had been implemented in preparation for implementation of the Education Reform Act 1988.

Apart from preparing for the Act, Kent as a county, led by the Chief Executive, Paul Sabin, was in the process of decentralizing its services. One reason for this was its geographical size, but another was the belief in the benefits of decentralization to financial control and service management. There was overall frustration with the LEA in schools and decentralization was seen as a way of dealing with this. Also, along with many other Conservative authorities, Kent Councillors felt that they should demonstrate support for the government by demonstrating that local financial management in schools could work.

We place schools in Kent between positions 5 and 6 on the spectrum. They are in competition with each other, and there is consumer choice of provider. However, this is still a restricted market because of the restrictions set on changing the product/service mix by the need to conform to the National Curriculum. There is also a degree of local political control by the LEA.

Our ninth and final example is London Buses Ltd (LBL), a subsidiary of London Transport (LT). Change in London Buses has been incremental but one significant event was an examination of LT by the Monopolies and Mergers Commission in 1980. Their report highlighted the need for increased productivity, efficiency, control, matching supply and demand, and clearly defined objectives. This partly led to the establishment of eight bus districts, but another impetus was the idea that LT was no longer value for money.

A further change was brought about by the London Regional Transport Act 1984, which replaced the former LT executive with London Regional Transport (LRT). It also transferred responsibility for London Transport from the GLC to the Department of Transport. One of the first requirements of LRT following the act was a duty to establish companies to run London bus and underground services and so LBL was set up in 1985. Bus routes were also opened up to tendering.

At the time of the research, the main operational control was exercised at individual garages. LBL is divided into eleven geographical subsidiaries plus London Coaches and Westlink. While each of these subsidiaries has a management board, the garage has primary responsibility for the service. Garages are the responsibility of Garage General Managers (GGMs).

LBL, as a subsidiary of London Regional Transport, receive a block grant from the Treasury via LT. Revenue, both on and off bus is also allocated. (On bus revenue is collected when the passenger pays for his/ her fare when boarding a bus, off-bus revenue is the money that goes to LT from the sale of travel cards, etc.) Once subsidiary companies receive their portion of the budget, they can decide on staffing levels and maintenance and engineering at the garage level. In other words the companies are not operated as completely independent businesses. Marketing and capital expenditure are still the responsibility of LT.

We place LBL at position 6 on the competitive spectrum because of the influence exerted on it through London Transport who are still accountable to the government. There is some competition for routes through a tendering process. Some people believe that the establishment of the eleven subsidiary bus companies is a preparation for further deregulation and eventual privatization. Management are required to think competitively, even though scope for new entrants is heavily regulated.

The organizations are placed on a spectrum in Figure 2.7.

In the next chapter we examine the range of possible competitive actions which might be taken by managers in these circumstances. It is apparent that in none of the examples studied would managers be expected to run their organizations as if they were businesses.

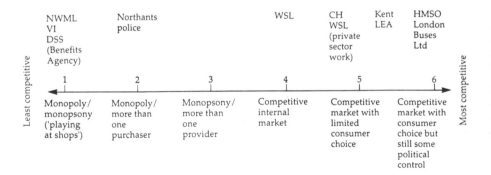

Figure 2.7   A competitive spectrum

3   Competitive behaviour

Introduction

It is clear from our analysis of the organizations we have studied that they range across the competitive spectrum. At one end there is no competition at all, rather an arm's length relationship between a purchaser and a provider. At the most competitive end, while politics still has influence (in the form of Government ownership, enabling legislation and so on), an organization may face both public and private sector competitors and supply its products and services to a range of organizations. So it is apparent already that introducing 'markets' to former public sector monopolies has a wide range of meanings.

Another important point is that the 'new' markets may not be new at all. For example, for seven of our sample (the five Executive Agencies, Northamptonshire Police and the Department of Social Security) the analysis reveals minor or marginal changes. In none of these cases are the changes sufficient to move any organization to a more competitive position on the spectrum.

In contrast, Kent schools and London Buses Ltd have been required to face more competition. Yet it is apparent from both the research and wider contact with public sector managers that market or competitive language is extensively used, in phrases such as 'being asked to compete with one hand tied behind our back' and 'no one owes us a living'. Managers and staff may *feel* that they are being asked to behave more competitively. Real competition can be an important stimulus to changed managerial behaviour and motivation and this is considered in this chapter.

So, the purpose of introducing competition is to change the behaviour of managers and workers. How does this work? First, there is an expectation that competition will exert a downward pressure on costs as the costs of services are first exposed and then compared with alternatives. Second, managers are expected to be more responsive either to the service user, often restyled the 'customer', or to an agent acting on the customers' behalf. The idea is that, by introducing a clear 'buyer–seller' relationship and giving the purchasers alternatives, the organizations will become more like businesses. Third, the vision of an external 'enemy' or competitor is designed to stimulate action to ensure survival, again becoming more 'business-like'.

However, the structural changes alone, whether major or minor, do not automatically transform organizations; the actual changes achieved are mediated through the managers' perceptions of their new circumstances. Some managers perceive themselves to be in competition but subsequently realize that little has changed and become demotivated. Others are keen to push back the regulatory boundaries as far as possible. Others are nervous of the changes and feel inadequate because of lack of training. Still others feel that basic provision in their field should be centrally funded as a matter of policy and that cost saving through competition is inadequate to make up for basic under-funding. So, just as a range of competitive options is being adopted, individual managers perceive them in a variety of ways.

The second element which will determine how the new structures produce change is the skill of the managers. Hospital managers do not automatically become expert competitive strategists overnight. Indeed many managers are at a loss about how to behave in the new markets: competition is often equated with price competition, as if price were the only criterion for choice. People engage in developing brand images (with the associated logos) and promoting them heavily before establishing the organization's position in the market. For some managers, of course, this may be the only real 'competitive' freedom that they have obtained.

A clear analysis of the changing market is of course necessary for the success of any business. Traditionally, in the public sector there have not been people who have had to be concerned about such matters. People are learning quickly but inevitably mistakes are being made. It is very difficult to predict the development of competition in a market, especially when deregulation produces new entrants and other shifts in structure. A good example is the deregulation of buses: many new entrants appeared in the early days, and then a series of mergers and acquisitions produced larger and larger groups.

In this chapter we look at the range of competitive behaviours which is being displayed. There are two elements to this: the competitive stance and the mechanisms used to enact the stance. At its simplest, competition may be based either on price or differentiation (making the product or service seem more valuable because it is in some way different from or better than other equivalents). Generally, organizations need to engage in price competition only where they cannot establish that their product or service is different from those of their competitors. It is normally more profitable to maintain high prices and persuade customers that the particular product, or brand, is more valuable than any others.

The mechanisms which managers can use to pursue these competitive stances in 'real' markets are the subjects of many large studies of corporate strategy. The range available in the public sector is rather more restricted than that used by companies. Certain mechanisms are ruled out: 'globalization' to establish world markets, for example, is not an option for public bodies; mergers and acquisitions to reduce the amount of competition has limited application; vertical integration is often impossible because of the institutional arrangements which are being established (e.g. an Executive Agency being vertically separated from its parent department).

This still leaves a range of competitive actions open in the new public sector markets, such as: pursuing new markets and customers; developing new products and services and dropping less valuable ones; changing the ways in which goods and services are produced; adjusting prices to take advantage of market conditions; and investment. We now consider each of these in turn.

Pursuing new markets and customers

One clear principle which has been adopted by the government when establishing some of the new competitive environments is that public agencies should not attempt to enter markets or pursue customers in which the private sector is currently operating.

For example, local authority Direct Labour Organizations (DLOs) are restricted to working for their own authority and for a specified set of other public sector bodies, a restriction which has been in place since 1963 (under the Local Government Goods and Services Act). Under competitive tendering success is dependent upon creating a steady flow of work, in order to sustain a workforce and to cover overheads. If the only acceptable tenders are for a very restricted range of clients, the DLOs are at a disadvantage against competitors who have a wider scope. For example, an authority which has a workforce engaged on street cleaning and refuse collection has only one chance of winning a contract. Its competitors have the opportunity of tendering for all the local authority contracts in the country.

The legislation on community care similarly places a severe restriction on the ability of local authority residential homes to compete with the private and voluntary sectors. If people are referred to a local authority home they are not entitled to the same income support as they would receive in a private home. The commercial logic facing local authorities is that they should dispose of their own residential establishments and exit from that sector of the market.

So far as the Executive Agencies in this study are concerned, the same general rules hold. They are bound by statutory duty: while they may offer additional services to meet customer demand where these services are close to their statutory obligations, they may not expand into competition with existing private sector suppliers.

This does not mean that they are not in competition. That is determined by the market position in which they found themselves at the time of adopting Agency status: that analysis is contained in Chapter 2. HMSO, therefore, has quite broad scope to enter new fields in its core business, because its existing scope is so wide. However, it may *not* expand to supply to the private sector. HMSO's monopoly has been removed (for nearly all of its business) so that it is opened to competition, but cannot offer similar competition in return. National Weights and Measures Laboratory, on the other hand, is permitting and encouraging private sector companies to take on more of some of its work (while retaining a monopoly on policy advice and certification) rather than enjoining a competitive fight. This situation may change with the advent of the single European market in 1992, when the Laboratory will find itself facing European competition.

Companies House Executive Agency continues to supply its company information direct to end users and to Agents who compete with it for the end-user market. It cannot choose to freeze out those competitors by refusing to supply them: it *is* permitted to offer an increasingly competitive threat by becoming more efficient. It may not expand its services to compete with the more sophisticated Agents, for example by analysing as well as simply supplying company information. It may introduce new services which are closely related to its core statutory functions which increase the level of competition it offers. Warren Spring Laboratory may seek to expand its customers base, but only to public sector bodies. Its private sector work is limited to 10% of turnover. Therefore the Laboratory is restricted in its competitive repertoire, while being opened up to competition through being required to distance itself from its parent Department, to complete service agreements with all its purchasers and to become more cost competitive.

Finally, the Vehicle Inspectorate is an excellent example of the difficulties which these carefully constructed, bureaucratic rules about competition can bring. It is a regulatory authority, a statutory monopoly: it licenses MOT testing stations and itself tests Heavy Goods Vehicles and Public Service Vehicles. On 18 March 1991, some vehicles (those with a design gross weight of 3500 kg or less) were reclassified to require an MOT, instead of a Heavy Goods Vehicle test. As Vehicle Inspectorate was already in this market, they are to be allowed to remain in it. This means that they will now be competing with their licensees, the MOT garages and stations. This does mean that managers will no longer have to act 'as if there were competition', because now there is some. However, it further exacerbates the existing dilemma facing this and so may other public sector service organizations. Added to the customer service/customer regulation dilemma, is the customer license/customer competition dilemma.

However, at the other end of our competitive scale competition is freer. For example, the newly independent Polytechnics, which have become corporate bodies, are in a very competitive market. As an increasing amount of funding for Polytechnics from the Polytechnic Central Funding Council (PCFC) is calculated on student numbers, the polytechnics have been encouraged to increase their numbers of students, in competition with each other and with the Universities. There is no restriction on the types of students, or their place of origin.

In other parts of the education service, open enrolment for secondary schools (introduced in the 1980 Education Act) means that, in principle, schools are forced to compete with each other. In effect schools are also competing with the private schools which pupils from their area could attend.

The NHS reforms introduce competition among units and between units and the private sector. The degree to which units are free to pursue patients depends partly on the sorts of services they provide. Clearly some services are more local than others: community services are, by their nature, local, while some specialities can attract patients from a national or international marketplace. Some hospitals target the international market for a proportion of their capacity in order to attract funds which otherwise they would not be able to obtain.

In all these examples, the freedom to compete is determined by two factors: the nature of the service and the regulations controlling competition. Some services are geographically restricted, especially if people have to travel from home to gain access to them. The rules generally seem to be based on the principle that if there is a well-developed private sector, the public providers will have limitations on their ability to pursue new customers. Where the private sector is currently small or in a poor position to compete then a more liberal regime will operate. This is the opposite of what might be expected from an ideology which favoured competition: the market would be expected to be the only regulator required if public bodies decided to behave commercially, since failure to compete would itself regulate the market.

For managers this can be frustrating: they may adopt both the language and the techniques of competition but still see the success of their organizations being jeopardized by regulation.

Developing new products and services

Most public agencies have statutory restrictions on the nature of their activities. Local authorities are governed by the *ultra vires* principle, which means that they may not perform functions for which there is no statute. Executive Agencies often have their statutory functions laid down in legislation: they now also have their operating rules specified in the Framework Agreement with their parent department. Health authorities may undertake income generation activities, but these are ancillary to their main healthcare tasks.

However, imaginative politicians and managers have developed new services. The growth of leisure provision by local authorities has been a result of a decision to change the 'product portfolio' of local authorities. This is especially striking in Northern Ireland where all but a small residual set of functions have been taken away from local authorities: there, leisure development thrives.

The Polytechnics have been able to develop new courses and different approaches to learning, through distance education and different modes of attendance. They have also experimented with new ways of delivering the service. They have, for example, been able to franchise activities to Further Education colleges and other providers of education. While improving access to education for people who would otherwise not be able to take advantage of the education service, these initiatives also have had a positive effect on Polytechnic finances.

Executive Agencies are encouraged and often required to earn a small portion of their income from new services. These services, as have been spelt out already, must be complementary to their statutory or required functions and must not take them into competition with the private sector. So Vehicle Inspectorate can now offer its statutory testing at different times, which may be more convenient to its users. Companies House offers faster (and more expensive) service by fax, but again this is simply a new version of existing business. These new services have different purposes: they encourage improved customer-focus; they reduce the need for central funding; and they are supposed to impact on the culture of the organization to make it more competitive-minded or business-like.

However, true freedom to diversify and enter new areas has normally come only through privatization. The decision by Severn Trent water company to buy a waste disposal company is an example of the freedom to add business areas which results from privatization: such a move would not have been possible under the previous Water Authority regime. Indeed, one of the main motivators for managers in the Water industry has been the opportunity to make more imaginative use of the assets of the companies, especially their land, than was possible before.

Changing the ways in which goods and services are produced

Technology

A major source of competitive advantage is the use of new technology to produce the same product or service. Airlines compete as much on their worldwide computer-based booking systems as on the network of routes. Bus companies compete by making sure that they have the right size and type of buses for each route. The deregulation of bus transport led to a much wider variety of types of buses being used.

The introduction of competition is not a necessary condition for managers to seek new technological solutions. For example, the Department of Social Security had begun its computerization of the benefits service before Agency status was even discussed. The Post Office introduced automatic sorting without the spur of competition.

The key condition to enable imaginative changes in technology is the freedom to invest. In the case of both the NHS and the Executive Agencies, there is still a high degree of Treasury control. However, changes are being made which are discussed more fully under 'Investment and Access to Capital Markets'.

Staff

The key resource of most public services is people. Managers need to be able to recruit, develop and retain the right staff if they are to be competitive. They are increasingly acquiring these freedoms: school governors and headteachers are recruiting their own staffs; national pay agreements are in some cases being bypassed so that local managers can establish their own pay regimes according to local circumstances.

However, much of this discretion has been given at a time when there has been a downward pressure on spending. Local agreements are substituted for national agreements to reduce cost, rather than to allow managers to be more flexible in their use of pay as a way of recruiting, motivating and retaining staff. Especially in the case of unskilled workers, competition has generally resulted in lower hourly rates of pay. At the other end of the scale managers have given themselves large pay rises, for example Chief Executives of NHS Trusts are paid on a far higher scale than the old Unit General Managers whom they replaced. Like the Managing Directors of the newly privatized industries they have justified their large salaries by comparison with the managers of other businesses of similar size or by saying that the 'market' rate is higher than the old scales.

Whether a manager of an NHS Trust would actually be able to command over £100 000 per annum in another industry has yet to be demonstrated.

There is some change for Executive Agencies too. The Treasury and the Office for the Minister for the Civil Service published a leaflet called 'Pay and Management Flexibilities', covering '40 selected flexibilities in the field of personnel management, pay and allowances' (when it was first published it contained only 25 flexibilities but was later expanded). Much play was made of the fact that these flexibilities had always been available to departments but little used. Also, the former Civil Service Commission, through which much recruitment into the Civil Service was centralized, has now itself become the Recruitment and Assessment Services Agency and now seeks to sell its services to Departments. Increasing levels of local recruitment and promotion are permitted within the Agencies. Many managers have complained to us about the lack of training to help them cope with their new 'freedoms'. It is interesting to recall that when the Department of Health devolved career development from Personnel to line managers, the policy faded because managers had no training in its execution.

Systems generally remain centralized for higher (grade 7 and above) grades, to allow free movement of such staff between areas. This 'free movement' means in practice that more senior managers can move from the Agency and back to the central Department. Movement *between* Departments has always been unusual in the Civil Service. Lower grades often do not seek mobility, for example clerical staff in Cardiff want a job at Companies House or some other local firm, not free movement between Cardiff, Edinburgh and London, working for Companies House. Civil Service grades have so far generally been left intact. HMSO is a major exception here, having slowly and painfully negotiated a new pay and grading regime with Treasury and Unions. Their new pay spine has four main 'grades' but many interim steps between. The Vehicle Inspectorate introduced a new grade 'Assistant Vehicle Examiner' to enable the use of fewer industrial staff.

Another new (and increasingly routinized) feature is bonus pay. Companies House, for example, reached its targets in its first year as an Agency and all staff received a £250 bonus. The Vehicle Inspectorate paid all staff a group bonus of £330 in 1989/90. Michael Bichard, Chief Executive of the Benefits Agency, told the Treasury and Civil Service Select Committee on 17 June 1991 that performance bonuses might be considered for his staff. So whether the Agency is trading or not, bonus payments may be set up. Civil Servants are used to basic pay and increments: volatile unconsolidated bonus payments are a change, the impact of which will be properly felt the first time a bonus is reduced or disappears.

The last area of notable change is that of performance related pay for the Chief Executives of Agencies. They are all coy about exactly how much they are paid especially after the 1991 furore about the salaries of the managers of newly privatized monopolies. We have no way of knowing: for example Nick Montagu, the Principal Establishment and Finance Officer of the Department of Social Security, refused categorically to make available the employment contract between the Chief Executive of the Benefits Agency and the Department when pressed to do so by the Treasury and Civil Service Select Committee.

What this means for the competitive stance of managers is that they are more able to compete on price, since in many cases they have the flexibility to bargain wages downwards, especially if they operate in parts of the labour market and areas of the country where national pay scales provide pay above the local going rate. What it does not do, however, is allow managers to use more imaginative Human Resource strategies to develop quality staff.

Prices

Price competition is the main consequence of introducing competitive tendering. Indeed, for those services provided by manual workers, a reduction in cost has been the main objective of competition policy.

The reforms in the NHS have been implemented to expose the high cost of certain treatments at some hospitals and drive their prices down. Purchasers with fixed budgets are expected to obtain the best value for money for those budgets. While it will take time for referral patterns to reflect relative prices, managers in the 'provider' side of the NHS are inevitably facing pressure to keep prices down.

So far, the education reforms have not produced price competition, except at the margin. Some schools are able to raise funds which allows them to offer extra activities without extra cost to the pupils. Keeping low charges, or reducing charges, for residential accommodation at Universities and Polytechnics may be a way of attracting students. Given that tuition fees are set nationally, this is at present one of the few flexibilities open to managers in manipulating price levels.

However, these tendencies are all towards lower prices. For the Executive Agencies in this study, our early research on their strategies (completed June 1990) showed that *whatever their competitive position*, their competitive stance was that of cost-cutting. Where no real market pressure existed, the Treasury intervened to set stiff value-for-money targets. Where there is evidence of markets really starting to operate, the Government intervenes to ensure that equity is maintained. For example, it was explicitly stated in the guidelines on implementation of the NHS reforms that hospitals should not exploit their market position to push prices up, either to make surpluses or to subsidize areas of work in which there was more competition. Then in early 1991, budget-holding GPs found that they were receiving faster treatment for their patients. Some hospitals, like King's College Hospital, Denmark Hill, London, had set themselves performance targets of keeping no budget holder GP's patient on the waiting list for more than a year. (Non-budget holding GPs' patients could expect to wait for anything up to three years at this hospital.) The hospital was also holding quality meetings every 4–6 weeks (getting 'closer to the customer') with budget-holding GPs. The Government stepped in to impose across-the-board service targets to guard against the emergence of a two-tier health system. The Royal Mail has a monopoly on the letter post for charges of less than £1: it is charged with making a surplus (£200 million in 1991/2) which it contributes to the Exchequer.

The rules are clear: managers can compete on price if this means that prices will be reduced. If the nature of the market is such that monopoly profits could be made, this is not allowed at all, or not allowed unless the profits are remitted to the Treasury.

Investment and access to capital markets

Liberalizing final product markets will not result in a change in resource allocation unless accompanied by a liberalization of capital markets. The freedom to make capital investments is an important tool to enable managers to implement changes in strategy. Normal rules of capital spending in the public sector are based on strict capital rationing: all capital expenditure counts against spending targets, whether the expenditure results in a cost saving or not. While the rules on capital spending for cost saving are being relaxed, in many cases the manager in the public sector is unable to take advantage of technical change to increase competitiveness. Investment decisions are not normally taken purely as a result of the examination of the 'business case': funds are rationed and allocated according to priorities which may have little to do with improving competitiveness.

However, some changes are being made. The major disincentives to carefully planned investment management for government departments have been annuality – the need to spend all finances within one year, often leading to end-of-year 'sprees' – and gross running cost control, meaning that finite cash is allocated on the basis of expected costs. These were important planks in keeping the Public Sector Borrowing Requirement under control. However, one and sometimes both of these constraints are removed for organizations becoming an Executive Agency. Trading Agencies (who actually sell their services direct to users) are often freed from gross running cost control, to allow new products and services to be offered, so long as they (at the very least) cover the cost of their provision. This new status is called being subject to Net Running Cost Control. In addition, some Agencies won agreements to carry budgets over from one year to the next (occasionally the parent Department, rather than Treasury, offer this 'buffer', as in the case of the Department of Trade and Industry and Companies House Executive Agency).

New Trading Fund legislation was enacted in 1990 to allow non-trading Agencies to benefit from these investment freedoms. The first Executive Agency, the Vehicle Inspectorate, became the first Trading Fund under this new legislation, on 1 April 1991. Sometimes the benefits, as in any change initiatives, are appreciated more in the long than the short term, as this extract from the Vehicle Inspectorate's 1991/2 Business Plan makes clear: '... this will be the first year of the Agency as a Trading Fund ... include an External Financing Limit (EFL)   of £2.3M ... The need to keep a light rein on expenditure and to provide a cash contingency within the EFL meant that capital expenditure originally planned for this period has been curtailed by deferring a number of capital projects'.

Net running cost control without freedom from annuality, and vice versa, can still feel extremely restricting for managers. A quotation from one manager in the Price Waterhouse Survey Report on Executive Agencies in March 1991 said: 'One net running costs Agency which is self-financing, sums it up by regretting "the need to surrender surplus receipts at 31 March every year and to start each year at 1 April as if we were a bankrupt company".'

Investment decisions which involve a change in direction are still subject to greater restrictions. For example, money raised from selling assets can rarely be used to fund continuing current expenditure. If a hospital wants to sell a site, for example, to enable it to provide care in the community for the people who would otherwise have been in hospital, the decision is not within the manager's discretion.

Changes in the competitive environment

Figures 2.1 to 2.6 represent different market structures in which managers might find themselves. The important question which will reveal whether their behaviour is likely to change is whether they have moved from one place in the competitive spectrum to another. If we conclude that competition can be a spur to greater efficiency, has the Executive Agency initiative actually moved any of the organizations in our sample along the competitive spectrum? For none of our examples has it done that, with the possible exception of Companies House, where managers have been encouraged to regard an important segment of their customers as the competition. However, it remains a monopoly and could crush its 'competition' by declining to supply these intermediary agencies. This change in managerial perception is not easy to achieve and can be demotivating. Mr Ron Oliver, Chief Executive of the Vehicle Inspectorate, says that one should act as if there *were* competition. This is not easy in the absence of real competition for managers at any level inside the organization. All the Agencies are required to make up shortfalls in central funding by providing new customer services at the margin, closely related to their statutory duties. However, for the statutory monopolies furthest towards the non-competitive end of the spectrum, the most this is intended to contribute is about 10% of income. This is not sufficient to shift the focus of the organization further along the spectrum towards competition. Further, Agencies which spend a greater proportion of their turnover than is warranted by the new income gained on trying to promote to this customer fringe risk disillusioning their workforce. This has been an issue concerning managers at the Building Research Establishment, where managers feel that extraordinary effort is being put into earning the 10% of private sector work which research establishments have been required to earn since the 1989 Review.

So the real question is, are any of these organizations being forced to compete with another potential provider of the service? If the market change maintains the monopoly, it is likely that managers will not be under any new or different pressure. They will still face the problem of living within a budget and facing outside scrutiny on their costs but these pressures have always been present.

Another important question might be, are they put into a different structural relationship with the service users? In many parts of the public sector there are campaigns to improve service to the public. These efforts are voluntary in the sense that it is not essential to attract customers or keep them happy. A monopoly provider of an essential service only needs to provide good service if they feel some sense of moral obligation or face imposed targets from their funders. The current reforms rely no longer on 'moral obligation' or public service values: they rely instead upon contracts and visible performance targets.

The purchasers' perspective

Dividing public sector organizations into purchasers and providers produces a large number of changes in job title. People who were nominally or actually in charge of running services now have a new role of planning for provision to meet need and specifying and commissioning the service.

Whether this enables the managers who are put into the purchaser role to perform their role effectively depends in large measure upon the training they receive and upon the amount of power they have in relation to the providers.

Market structure is thus an important factor. If the purchaser faces a range of suppliers the task is easier than negotiating with a monopoly. On the other hand, the providers are in a strong position in relation to the purchaser if there is no spare capacity in the system because the purchaser will have to be satisfied with whatever can be obtained. The purchaser's apparent choice is illusory if there are many waiting in line and thus there is significant excess demand.

The other aspect of market structure is the *number* of purchasers. If providers face a number of purchasers, the purchasers may need to seek to place themselves in a stronger position because of their excess demand. For example, health authorities have realized that competition among purchasers puts them in a weak position and have established purchasing consortia to strengthen their hand. In the Civil Service, there are not always alternative purchasers except, for example, in those cases where services are provided in exchange for cash. Thus HMSO operates in the face of a large number of purchasers who in turn have a choice of supplier.

In the case of the large Agencies, Benefits and Employment, the relationship between purchaser and provider is that of a monopoly facing a monopsony, 'bilateral monopoly', or position 1 on the competitive spectrum in Chapter 2. The same condition applies, for example, in areas of the country where there is only one General Hospital and one District Health Authority within reasonable travelling distance. Specialist services in social services may often be in the same position. This is a very special case of market structure. There are no competitive forces which drive the two parties towards an agreement on price or on the specification of services.

What might be expected to happen in these special markets? Purchasers are under a variety of 'old' pressures from the people funding the service, including an expectation that productivity will increase and a responsibility for achieving value for money and they will therefore tend to seek as low a price as possible, to maximize the amount of service produced for the available budget. In the absence of comparative prices, they only have recourse to information about the costs incurred by the providers. It is in the interests of the providers to inflate their apparent costs to maximize their own revenue. Since purchasers are subject to an annual budget, an annual negotiation needs to take place on the amount of money to be made available to the provider. This annual bargaining makes it essential that the purchaser has a detailed knowledge of the cost structure of the provider. Because of this the exchange of information between the two organizations needs to be significant and will tend to bring the two parties close together. In effect the purchasers will tend to have an interest in the internal management of the providers. They will attempt to exercise this interest through the form of contract which is produced. The contracts will therefore not only be concerned with the outputs of the providers but also, especially in people-intensive services, with the number of employees, their grades and their working methods.

The other pressure towards this close involvement comes from the providers of the funders. The Treasury or the local authority Finance Committee will attempt to protect itself against the power of the monopoly provider by maintaining detailed scrutiny of their costs and working methods. For managers in the newly formed provider units, this can be very frustrating.

Whatever the market structure the purchaser's role in the market requires them to establish mechanisms for monitoring and controlling the provision of the services. In Social Services, authorities have been required to establish independent Inspection Units which will monitor standards of care. In Social Security, like all the Executive Agencies, a set of indicators has been established with specific targets set, in their case on the speed and accuracy with which claims are processed. Often monopoly providers are already subject to such scrutiny as part of their control mechanisms, for example Companies House and the Companies House Users Group (which prevented them from closing their London office through its lobbying activities).

These mechanisms will in part determine how managers on the 'purchasing' side of the organizations behave. If the mechanisms are based on performance indicators which are calculated from data collected by the providers, the purchasing role is likely to be slight, in between the annual price and volume negotiations. Indeed, the rumps of departments have been told to slim down to reflect this diminished role. Often, however, monitoring takes place quarterly in addition to the annual negotiating role, again boosting the power of the purchaser and furnishing a further source of frustration for the provider. There are many reasons for this: lack of adequate performance measures and an inability to 'let go' of former hierarchical relationships are two frequent causes.

The other element of pressure on the purchasers in the new markets is the service users. Figure 2.6 shows an ambiguous relationship between purchasers, providers and users. In principle, the task of service purchasers is to plan for service provision by finding out the needs for service, and by ensuring the provision. However, the day-to-day contacts in the service relationship are between the *providers* and the users. The problem for the purchasers is how to collect information from those exchanges in a manner which can inform about the way in which services are specified and provided. In turn, the providers may find better or more 'customer-oriented' ways of producing services. They then have to persuade the purchasers to include the new provisions in their purchasing plans and practices.

The real problems are how to cope with innovation and how to decide what scale of turnover is acceptable. Some innovations will inevitably emerge from the daily practice of providers. In the case of social services, service developments have occurred as individual social workers or other staff have developed better ways of providing care for clients. If purchasers are remote from such developments they may be tempted to disallow them as being outside the contract or they may be so radical that they would require ratification by Parliament. Conversely, if the purchasers wish to promote innovation, they have no daily experience on which to base improvements.

The service users' perspective

All of these changes could be completely opaque to a service user. If the services are provided by contracts between purchasers and providers without the involvement of the users, from their point of view they might face an identical exchange to the one they had before.

Choice

Even if the purchaser has established a market in which there is a choice of supplier, this choice may not be made available to the service user. For example, when local authority social services departments contract with the voluntary or private sectors for the provision of community care, the person who needs the service may still be faced with no choice of provider. Similarly in the NHS, patients are restricted in the choice of hospital to those with which their health authority or general practitioner has a contract.

Clearly where no competition is established by the new arrangements, choice is unaffected. The Benefits Agency is still a monopoly supplier of social security benefits and, as yet, claimants do not even have a choice of which local office to approach. In those cases in which a monopoly is sustained the organization has to use levers other than competition if it wants to change managers' and workers' behaviour. Those which have emerged from our research are set out in Chapter 7.

Other means of influence

In the absence of choice, the users of public services would also need alternative means of making their wishes heard by service providers. The Inland Revenue has produced a Taxpayers' Charter, which sets out in general terms the standard of service which can be expected. The Conservative Government announced in 1991 its plans for a Citizen's Charter which would do the same for a range of other public services, developing the approach taken by local authorities such as the City of York and the London Borough of Islington.

These approaches emphasize the service users' rights and entitlements as citizens rather than customers. If power for service users is not to be achieved through their ability to choose and to withhold their custom from a particular provider, such agreements are a useful mechanism.

However, they depend upon the purchasers' or providers' willingness to define the standards of the existing service. They do *not* allow the citizens to determine the overall level of expenditure devoted to that service or the quality and quantity of the services to be provided. The democratic process is the main alternative source of influence. In the case of most services the mechanisms of democracy are imperfect for this task. Even in local government the connection between voting and the level of expenditure and standards of service is weak. In the case of services provided by the NHS and the Civil Service the lines of choice and accountability are so stretched that no individual citizen can have much influence.

Regulatory bodies, user groups and well-developed complaints pro-cedures may form an alternative source of influence. However, these mechanisms are not very publicly accessible or visible in the UK. They do not form a strong, collective alternative to individual market power.

Thus, it is important to distinguish between 'choice' which is available to customers in a competitive market and 'choice' available to users of public services. In a market in which the customers have purchasing power, choice and influence are proportional to the amount of money that the customer has. By definition, richer customers have more choice than poor ones. If public sector markets are not to generate privileged groups of service recipients, either everybody has to have access to the same amount of purchasing power according to their need for the service, or mechanisms other than markets should be used for the distribution of services. One way to achieve this is the current form of rationing according to an accepted definition of need. An extension of this idea might be to give the public sector customer choice by allocating a voucher expressing the assessed individual level of need. The choice, however, still remains at the level of choosing among service providers, rather than influencing the primary definition of need.

Although the Benefits Agency is a monopoly provider, the beneficiaries can be offered a choice of methods of applying for benefit (personal interview, telephone, post). Michael Bichard, the Chief Executive of the Benefits Agency, wants to run the service in such a way that customers will be able to choose which office to visit: 'we want to move towards claimants going to the office of their choice ... we need to find out what our customers want from us and the priorities they place on us' (verbal evidence to the Treasury and Civil Service Select Committee 17 June 1991). Pupils can choose which school to attend without entering market transactions in the sense of paying for the service.

Of course, some services are simply not susceptible to a cash transaction analogous to that between a customer and a service provider. The relationship between a department whose task is to deliver social security benefits and its beneficiaries is not equivalent to a 'customer' relationship. Withholding custom hurts only the customer.

There is little doubt, from our and others' research, that competition can be a spur to increased efficiency, if it is perceived as real. It can stimulate managers to pursue objectives such as lower costs and a more responsive service, even accepting the limitation that the stimulus is generally towards marginal changes in the existing services rather than towards radical change. In the next chapter we examine decentralization as one such mechanism. In Chapter 7 we consider others which emerged from the research.

4 Decentralization

In the previous chapter we saw that, even without a fully competitive environment, public sector managers have seized varying degrees of managerial autonomy. There has been a tendency towards pushing accountability for performance and resource use further down the organizations of the public sector. Thus decentralization can be used, with or without the accompaniment of competition, as a method of revitalizing managerial motivation and of improving service to the customer or user.

Decentralization in the public sector has reflected a trend in the private sector over the past two decades. Many companies have tried to reduce the size of their head offices and make plant and branch managers more autonomous, while supplying them with the support and help to get on and do their job.

> When Michael Edwardes took over as Chairman of British Leyland in 1977 he set about reducing the size of the headquarters. 'On my rare visits there I found no enthusiasm and a stifling atmosphere, rather like being in a luxury liner without portholes; corridors between closed doors, behind which people seemed to work in a vacuum, at least two steps removed from the "nuts and bolts" of the business ... the centralised concept disturbed me, for it wasn't only cost we were determined to save, but the knock-on effect of bureaucracy: the "second-guessing" of Cars headquarters in Coventry and of Commercial Vehicles, centred at Leyland ...'

This distrust of centralized bureaucracies applied not only to the nationalized industries and big companies but also to large public sector organizations. In social services departments in local authorities, for example, many Directors decided that authority should be pushed down the organization. (see Young and Hadley, 1990). They thought that only local managers would know best how to allocate resources in a way which was sensitive to local people's needs. Centrally based rules and allocation decisions might produce a standardized service rather than local responsiveness.

Why decentralize?

The first aspect we need to consider is the reason for decentralizing. One motivation for decentralization was to close the gap between 'centre' of the organization and the business of producing and selling goods and services. A plant manager, for example, who always has to refer upwards decisions about investment or operations management is likely to be demotivated. People who are dependent on the hierarchy above them become administrators of other people's ideas rather than managers. The corollary of lack of management responsibility at lower levels is that the jobs which people are doing further up the hierarchy become impossible. Decisions have to be made without direct experience of the consequences.

A second motivation was to save money. Throughout the private sector the recession at the beginning of the 1980s made companies look for reductions in cost. One source of cost was the large headquarters staffs who, in the short term at least, seem to make little direct contribution to profitability. Similar 'shake-outs' occurred as the 1990 recession started. These cost saving exercises should not be confused with making organizational changes for operational or strategic reasons.

Reductions in senior and middle level staff were facilitated by increasing use of information technology which reduced the need for large numbers of people scrutinizing and checking the actions of others. This allowed layers of supervisory management to be removed. Middle managers' roles had consisted of passing instructions downwards and information upwards. More direct information flows have removed the need for many such information conduits.

Getting 'close to the customer' was also a popular slogan of the 1980s, the idea that managers should not only be close to the action in the sense of where production or service delivery actually takes place, but also should listen to and understand what customers want. So a third motivation was to render management decisions more local, to increase the chances of those decisions reflecting customers' preferences. The remoteness of head office and senior staff from the market place was seen as a major reason for poor performance.

All these ideas were closely linked, in that the process of tightening financial control was also thought to be easier if managers at relatively low levels of the hierarchy are held to account for spending. Hence decentralization not only saves the costs of headquarters, it also makes budgetary control more effective.

Thus, there was a trend towards more delegation and a more decentralized style of management. However, the term 'decentralization' covers a variety of managerial changes. The changes in the management of the Civil Service as a result of the Next Steps initiative might be described as decentralization from departments to Executive Agencies. However, this only necessarily implies a delegation of authority from a Permanent Secretary to an Agency Chief Executive. Delegation within an Executive Agency is not an essential part of the reforms. So, for example, the Chief

Executive of the Benefits Agency could run a centralized organization through a hierarchy or could delegate authority to Branches or beyond.

In the Education service, authority has been delegated to schools through the Local Management Schemes of the Education Reform Act 1988. Clearly the level of delegation here is to relatively small units, compared with the 70 000 employees of the Benefits Agency. However, the principles are the same: a management unit with authority and accountability; cutting out hierarchy; budgets which are cash limited.

A simple impetus for decentralization has been the size of area over which an organization has to operate. While control can be exercised from a central point, it is often easier to split managerial control into geographical areas.

Decentralization and performance measurement

An important second aspect is the enhanced use of performance measurement under decentralized management. Whatever the motivation for decentralization, senior management cannot afford to allow people lower down the organization to have so much autonomy that they fail to follow the strategy of the organization or meet agreed performance targets. Decentralization requires an adequate system to measure the performance of units and their contribution to the performance of the organization as a whole. Performance measurement can either be used as a tool for control, especially financial, or more positively to allow managers and others to know how well they are doing.

There are various elements of performance which can be measured, ranging from simple measures of resources used or inputs, through measures of the service delivery process and the volume of outputs, to attempts to measure the *outcomes* achieved by the services. Different people are interested in different aspects: senior management may be more interested in resource use than service users are. People engaged in service design will be interested in qualitative measurements of user reaction to services.

In some cases people use an aggregate measure to encompass everything. For example, London Buses Ltd calculates a percentage mileage statistic for each route, which includes a measure of how many buses are available and in what condition. This provides an indicator of the effectiveness of the organization in getting good buses on the road.

Some performance targets are imposed from outside. For example, each Executive Agency has an agreed set of targets which are written into its Framework Document. These are negotiated with the parent department and endorsed by the minister. The broad aims are often fixed by statute:

the detailed performance objectives are about how the statutory targets are met. Looking back to the Ibbs Report, we can extract what might be called the Treasury definition of success: '... to deliver services more efficiently ... for the benefit of taxpayers'.

With this as a baseline we can try to track improvements by starting with the Framework Documents. In fact, not all of these included specific performance measures (as opposed to broad aims) and, as it happens, none of our sample did. We have to look at the Annual Reports since then to find performance measures. All of these are published but, like many sets of company accounts, the basis for measurement and the things being measured may vary from year to year so that it is not always possible, as an outside observer, to keep track of improvements. The performance setting mechanism between Minister and Agency is not visible: but it is possible, with a little effort, to track crudely the performance measures over time.

Given this proviso, we can say that some of these five agencies have achieved more of their targets than others; that none appear to have achieved all their targets; and that it is usually possible to find some written explanation for underachievement of objectives. For example, the Vehicle Inspectorate's Framework Document states: '3)a) (the Inspectorate) will be expected to achieve the objectives and targets set by the Ministers and the Department'. Their Annual Reports set out most performance indicators clearly in graph and tabular form: in 1988/9, they achieved only one out of five service targets 'due to staff shortages'. The National Weights and Measures Laboratory again reports its performance measures very clearly in Annex 2 of its 1989/90 Annual Report: it achieved five out of nine objectives that year. Interestingly, Wendi Harrison, of the Council for Civil Service Unions, points out that in July 1991, of 2000 targets set by Next Steps Agencies, only 20 are qualitative.

Some organizations have better developed performance measures than others. Generally measures used for control are imposed by the centre, while those measures which are about the quality of service are more likely to be developed locally. One Area Manager in Kent said: 'there is no point in the LEA imposing performance indicators; there are some things that need to be built up from school level so that they can feel ownership of them ... building up PIs is a process of consultation'.

This is a general principle which might be applied to all performance measurement in a decentralized structure. A Senior Executive Officer in one of the five Agencies said: 'each area of activity is different but is covered by the same measures. For instance Area A is demand-led and time consuming: the Area B Branch is not. But staff in both areas are subject to the same calculation. Therefore Area A does not appear to be reaching targets' (interview). Had the targets been agreed with this manager they would have been more relevant as a managerial tool, rather than as an ineffective control mechanism.

A second principle is that there should be a small number of measures and targets. Mike Fogden, formerly a Grade 3 at the Department of Employment and the first Chief Executive of the Employment Services Executive Agency, was quoted in *The Times* Newspaper of 10 April 1991 as saying that the Agency had been given targets for management, whereas Whitehall used to measure activities rather than output. 'We counted everything that moved. We had 120 performance measurements, which, of course, no one focused on.'

The third principle is that the measurements and targets should be widely known and highly visible. People cannot be motivated by targets which only appear when the Annual Report is written.

If these principles are applied, performance measurement can be an integral part of a delegated management process. If they are not, the measures will remain at best an occasional irritant as they are scrutinized by outsiders.

Delegating what?

The third aspect which needs to be made clear is exactly *what* is being delegated. There are marked differences among public services when we ask this question. A minimal approach is the delegation of *accountability for spending.* Budgetary control in Education is now largely handled at School and College level. The Financial Management Initiative in the Civil Service, the precursor of the Next Steps initiative, was mainly concerned with holding more middle managers accountable for their budgets. The reforms of the NHS have exposed individual units to financial pressure to break even, without a safety net of a higher level authority to get them out of financial difficulties.

Managers are usually more willing and better able to keep within budgets, as they have of meeting performance targets, if they have *an involvement in setting the budget.* Managers regard arbitrary budgets which have been handed down to them with scepticism. This dimension of decentralization does not necessarily imply a high degree of managerial discretion. It is possible for managers at a lower level to have responsibility for the detail of constructing their budgets without having much control over the way in which money is spent.

Significant control arises if managers have the discretion to vary the ways in which money is spent, especially on the choices about the mixture of types of inputs to be used, or the 'production function'. If managers can substitute capital for labour, or can switch one sort of labour for another to achieve the same outputs, they have real control over their resources. If they do not have such control, even if they are charged with constructing the budget and monitoring expenditure, they still have the use of their resources dictated from above. So, for example, while some Executive Agencies have gained some limited freedom to transfer between budgets, often even these freedoms are held at higher levels in the organization. One interviewee told us: 'A torch for looking at a vehicle is Miscellaneous Minor Equipment, whereas for a power cut it is Miscellaneous Minor Expenditure.'

An International Monetary Fund paper (IMF, 1988) on input controls suggested principals may still wish to control the inputs used by agents because managers in the agencies wish to spend money on certain inputs, especially staff, for reasons of their own self-interest rather than efficiency. They suggest that delegation of input controls may become more popular if:

1   The size and complexity of the agencies make the detailed control of inputs by the principals impossible
    or
2   Methods other than input controls have been found to monitor the performance of the agencies.

The same arguments apply to delegation within an agency: hierarchical control over inputs may be a suitable method of control if efficiency or effectiveness are difficult to measure. On the other hand, if it is not possible to judge a junior manager's efficient or otherwise use of resources, the same problem applies at the higher level.

The fourth aspect of devolved management is the choice of products or services which the organization provides. In the public sector nobody has complete authority over these decisions because the organizations are governed by statute. However, at the margins there are significant choices to be made. In the police force, there are choices about how much resource to apply to traffic patrols, crime prevention and detection. These are different services which make distinct contributions to the well-being of the population.

In the Education service a large proportion of the 'product' is determined by the national curriculum but there is still discretion over what other academic subjects are taught and what extra-curricular activities are undertaken. There has always been a large degree of autonomy at school level over these professional matters which are subject to influence from outside mainly through the process of inspection.

The degree of discretion given to local managers about whom they should serve is partly determined by the overall rules governing the agency. In many cases, such as most of social security, there are national eligibility criteria which have to be followed at local level. However, the allocation of time to particular categories of case can have a significant impact on the level of service which different groups of claimants perceive themselves to receive.

In other cases, the system is designed to be discretionary. Although everyone has access to health care, there is automatically a rationing process which applies to all but the most acute cases. How that rationing operates and who makes the rationing choices is an important aspect of local discretion.

The degree of local autonomy in choosing which individuals shall or shall not receive a service is very important to individual service users. The term 'street level bureaucrat' has been used to describe the strategic shifts which can be made through exercising local autonomy. The desire to achieve consistency of access to services across the country is an important motivator for not decentralizing these decisions. For example, the Benefits Agency wants to create equal treatment for all claimants, or 'customers'. One mechanism which contributes to this is the 'integrated complementing system', a central control over the numbers of people employed in each office.

In each of the organizations that we examined there was an intention to delegate managerial control. For example, in April 1991, Her Majesty's Stationery Office Executive Agency implemented a restructuring initiative to 'delayer' the organization to four levels. This is designed to eliminate duplication and to increase even further internal delegation and has been closely watched in Whitehall. We now consider how far each organization in our research has been able to achieve the objective of increased delegation.

First we need to ask why the organizations embarked on their decentralizations. In all the cases there was an awareness of the need for efficiency and improved financial management. The general drive towards financial management across the public sector led to the development of systems of cost centre management, which in themselves necessarily imply a certain degree of decentralization. Even if there were no other motive for decentralizing, budget holders were expected to exercise financial control. Physical evidence of this most basic form of decentralization should manifest itself with attempts to establish some method of unit costing low down the hierarchy and with the contraction of the former centres, the HQs, their personnel and their functions. However, as the IMF said (1988): 'The rationale for decentralised operational decision making is that line managers have better information than the centre to adjust the input mix to improve services to clients and to lower costs than the centre.' (p72)

There were also some differences among the organizations we studied.

Northamptonshire Police

Northamptonshire police achieved a high level of decentralization except for budget making and budgetary control. When Maurice Buck was appointed Chief Constable in 1982, he took over what one senior officer described as a 'sub-standard force'. It also shared the characteristics of many other police forces including a traditional hierarchical structure; no statements of policy; no setting of objectives; no evaluation process; little financial management; little consultation; little systematic or long-term planning; minimal questioning of accountability; and powerful Chief Constables. Police managers had little or no incentive to concern themselves with the costs of the services that they provided. It was usually the Chief Constable who made decisions on increases in personnel or other inputs.

Buck gradually changed the force by introducing 'policing by objectives' (see Chapter 2). Lubans and Edgar, the authors of *Policing by Objectives* (PBO) were invited by Buck to talk to his officers and persuade them of the value of PBO.

The aims of PBO are as follows: 'It seeks to promote dynamism within the organisation, it devolves responsibility for setting and working towards objectives to managers at each level in the hierarchy, and it encourages participation and feedback from the bottom level of the organisation' (Horton and Smith, 1988).

It was justified on the grounds that the force could achieve better value for money based on ideas of efficiency and effectiveness. The process implies accountability for actions at both subdivisional level and within individual stations.

Although PBO did not necessarily involve devolved budgetary control, it was a logical next step when Circular 114/1983 was issued by the Home Office. This circular said that personnel increases would only be allowed if a force could demonstrate the efficiency with which existing personnel were used. Although not a financial circular, improved financial management and better management information were a necessary prerequisite for demonstrating efficiency and economy. Improved financial management implied in turn the establishment of cost centres and the gradual devolution of budget headings began. It seemed that budgetary control was a natural development of a reorganized force providing 'cost effectiveness' as well as the need to satisfy the Home Office that resources were being used efficiently.

The process was successful not simply because of Buck's commitment, but also because of a heavy input of training and the fact that the force was relatively small. The force was receptive to changes because Buck was new and there was a large turnover of senior officers soon after his arrival.

However, the service mix was not very devolved. There are many statutory constraints and general expectations on any police force which imply that a certain range of services is provided. The service mix is adjusted at the margin.

In reality, there is limited managerial discretion at the subdivisional level, which in turn, has consequences for decisions made over the production function. If the subdivisional commander has limited financial discretion, then he or she will be limited in the choices that can be made over inputs, especially people or technology. One instance concerned a communications room and the problem of 'incident logging', which is done manually and is therefore labour intensive. One commander decided that the solution was to have a slave computer for the staff to input information when they had a spare moment. The intention was to pay for this from the furniture budget but HQ were against the idea because it was outside the overall force strategy and the decision making system was unable to cope with such an innovation.

As well as involving officers in formulating force policy, decentralization has given officers a substantially different role. One officer commented that: 'some claim to want devolvement but they may not like it when they get it as there is little scope in which to hide'. The success or otherwise of the system seems to rest on the acceptance by officers of their new responsibilities.

However, at the operational level, although decentralization and PBO has given more autonomy to the subdivisions, it has also created seven or eight 'mini-forces' when, in the words of a senior officer, it should be 'the force, as a whole', that 'needs to be sold'. With the help of the subdivisions, the centre still needs to set the overall policy framework, enshrined in the Chief Constable's Policy Statement.

One senior officer describes how decentralization was 'more evident' in one subdivision. There, the superintendent had developed wider consultative procedures which he tried to continue on promotion to another subdivision: 'devolved management depended very much on the personalities involved; a superintendent has to trust his deputy'. In his new post, he set about widening the management team to involve civilian staff, Police Federation representatives and sergeants.

When he returned to the previous subdivision as commander, he was able to supply an example of the importance of the relationship with colleagues: 'I was faced with a particularly nasty racial issue and I expected my deputy to have a grasp of the situation, but because the previous superintendent had been personally involved, there had been no "carry over" on the community relations side. From this an objective emerged and the deputy was allowed to get into joint leadership. However, he found this difficult because he had been poorly motivated in the past.'

Another problem was that the expectations he had of his inspectors were too high. They appeared not to be accepting the levels of responsibility being given to them. From this, he developed the idea of a 'unique contribution', that each inspector had his own part of the operation that was his particular responsibility in the rolling inspection programme. Further, each layer of the organization had its own unique contribution to make. Sergeants should set standards among their other responsibilities; inspectors must plan and test the system; superintendents should set the objectives and 'provide the vision'. Self-inspection was an important innovation, recognizing as it does the importance of giving staff regular feedback rather than waiting for the annual inspection.

Decentralization was generally welcomed in the force: 'I like to think that devolved management has improved the service we give to the public although we know that we cannot be good at everything. We are in the process of prioritizing in trying to respond in a measured way with policing by objectives. Also, people respond better in a better managed environment' (interview).

The credibility of the decentralization process is underlined by the fact that under-performing subdivisions may see officers being removed for consistent underachievement of objectives.

The amount of managerial discretion that has been decentralized in the force has been sufficient to lead to a general agreement among the officers that service to the public has 'improved immeasurably', based on evidence from their sample surveys. We have been unable to independently verify this. Subdivisions have been able to divert resources to improve the overall efficiency of policing.

Figure 4.1 illustrates the elements of the Northamptonshire Police decentralization.

Kent Education Authority

Kent LEA responded early to the proposals for the Education Reform Act 1989 by preparing for Local Management of Schools (LMS), which involves financial delegation, or decentralized budgeting. The DES, in a draft consultative document stated that: 'The underlying principle of schemes of financial delegation is to secure the maximum delegation of financial and managerial power to governing bodies (of schools).'

In the schools there was frustration about the previous culture of financial management. For example, one headteacher said: 'I had always been frustrated at the lack of financial control: there always seemed to be people painting classrooms but there was no money for books. At the end

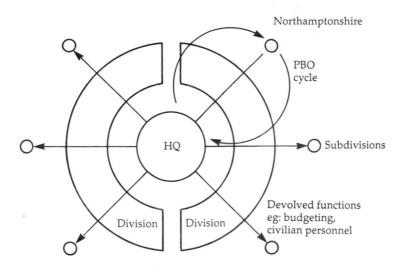

Figure 4.1   Northamptonshire police

of the financial year, I was always being told to spend up by tomorrow'
(interview).

Along with many other Conservative authorities Kent councillors felt
that they should demonstrate support for the government by showing
that local financial management can work. This lead to the pilot scheme,
ahead of LMS.

Budget making and financial control were genuinely devolved to
schools with relatively few constraints. This allowed schools to vary the
inputs, switching money from staffing to other items and to have a great
deal of freedom to adjust the ways in which the staffing budgets are spent.
Some costs are fixed, such as the rates bill. Also schools are unable to
depart from national pay scales but are free to use incentive allowances as
they wish.

The main constraint on the product/service mix is the national
curriculum, which accounts for about 75% of the time spent in schools. The
rest of the time spent is at the school's discretion.

Physical evidence of the decentralization has occurred at Springfield, the
LEA's HQ and 'centre'. Decentralization has reduced the number of staff
working at Springfield by around 50%. Also, three new posts were created:
Heads of Operations, Strategy, and Quality Assurance whose incumbents
have no line management function. Many of the HQs functions have been
devolved to six Area Offices which provide support services to the

schools, whose independence is not compromised because they have the
choice to go elsewhere for these services if they wish.

One headteacher summarizes the decentralization in Kent: 'LMS has
made a real difference to education all round. We see the educational
experience as a total, and we can now control all aspects.'

Figure 4.2 illustrates the relationships in Kent's devolved management
structure.

In Kent LEA, one of the 'heads of profession' stated that two of the
underlying principles of the decentralization were 'clear lines of accountability' and 'decisions at the point of service delivery'. Generally, headteachers favoured this approach and welcomed the freedoms afforded to
them in the decentralization. Furthermore, an internal market was established with the creation of Area Offices, who would sell support services
to the schools such as personnel management, financial management,
property and land maintenance, school meals and curriculum support. The
head of profession remains at the centre but accountability for these
services stops at the Area Office. Also, the heads of profession have no
line management function: 'Some may feel it as a loss of status ... we have

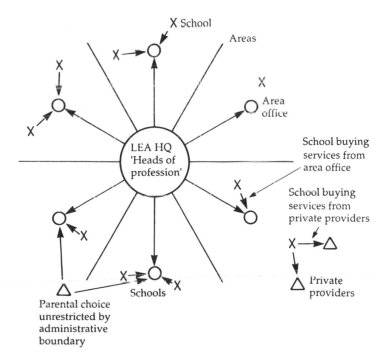

Figure 4.2   Kent local education authority

attempted to substitute influence and leadership for line management and different skills are needed.'

The difference is that the centre will now have to respond to ideas from the schools; not vice versa. Area services will also have to justify what they actually do for the school: for instance, they will be able to question the daily cost of an inspector. Kent LEA has seen a large-scale decentralization of staff to the area offices that provide the services to the schools. This has included the creation of new posts such as Customer Services manager in each area office whose main areas of responsibility are: educational psychology service; careers service; integrated support service; hearing impaired service; and allocation of school places. One Customer Services manager commented that: 'We are now in the market place, and if the service isn't up to scratch, then we will go out of business. It is possible that the schools can opt out and buy in support services from elsewhere, such as from a firm of local accountants.'

It is not just at the Area Offices where the changes have been felt, there has been considerable alterations in the way the schools are run. Headteachers described how their jobs have changed with decentralization. One stated that he needed to be more conscious not only of marketing but of society changing; of developments in education; of more administration; of more communication with parents; and of more involvement with inspectors and advisers. Then there are repercussions for the staff: '... we have had to structure the staff's time. Every morning, I have a senior staff meeting; and a Head of Departments and a Heads of Year meeting once a month. This has all brought pressure on the staff. With the (Education Reform) Act and the review of curriculum, staff have had to read documents, analyse themselves and give feedback. I have had to oversee all this ...'

Another head also said that staff time had to be organized and structured carefully, with particular attention being paid to the length and frequency of meetings. The result was that he was satisfied that they now had a more efficient and effective management structure with many teachers keeping records of non-teaching time spent. One comment was that: 'The new style head will have to delegate responsibility and have confidence in their staff.'

Like the Northamptonshire Police, meaningful decentralization at the school level seems to depend on the personalities and the size of the school involved. Another headteacher remarked that he didn't delegate within the school: all the work was done entirely by him and his secretary. He is also 'certain' that he can run the school more efficiently than the LEA. On the other hand, another school had appointed a full-time bursar, and they were confident about raising the money to fund the post.

Teachers said they had difficulty in analysing the impact this will have on pupils and parents and there was a belief that too much was being asked of both parents and teachers. One headteacher, for instance, because he had seen the problems his staff had in dealing with all the literature associated with reorganization at the same time as his senior staff taking on extra work, was 'almost scared to ask any more of them'. One head reported that many of his colleagues who had not been part of the pilot scheme prior to LMS would have difficulty in adjusting to the changes.

Some realize the implications of competition will mean that schools may close. Publication of school results may force closure of certain schools and although results may be the only, albeit contentious, measure of how good a school is, there is still the need 'to develop publicity and present the school to the community'. All this will have potentially serious implications for the delivery of the education service.

The Executive Agencies

Very different pictures emerged for the five Agencies in our research. As we mentioned at the start of this chapter, there are two different levels of decentralization. One is from Headquarters to the Agency itself: the second is downwards inside the Agency. Chapter Two sets out the delegated authority given to the Executive Agencies in theory. In this chapter, we look at how far *within* the Agencies these freedoms have been delegated down the line in practice.

Staff at the National Weights and Measures Laboratory were, in general, aware of the changes that Agency status had brought, primarily some end-year financial flexibility and some personnel delegations. Most staff were, however, unaware of the details of the changes and used new delegated authority little, if at all, considering this to be in the domain of 'management', who were presumed to wield the delegations on behalf of the organization. Most people felt that the change to Agency status had little impact. They saw themselves as members of a small unit which had always had its own identity. Professional, scientific independence was more valued than financial responsibility. There was a sense of still being controlled by the Department of Trade and Industry, but there was no evidence of any particular desire to change that.

This Agency felt not so much centralized — with 50 staff it is hard to imagine how this might be — as to operate from a scientific rather than a managerial culture. As one interviewee said, 'If an Agency is supposed to be much more like a business, there is a considerable gap.' Budget responsibility was mostly confined to recommending expenditure which 'managers and administration people' collate, approve and monitor.

Performance measures seemed to have the same purpose. There was general awareness that non-mobile staff can be recruited locally.

The picture was quite different at HMSO, although again Agency status was felt to have had little impact on the organization. The major organizational change for HMSO came in 1980, with the move to Trading Fund status. However, becoming an Agency was seen by some as a catalyst for the restructuring exercise which was implemented in April 1991. There is a clear business culture in HMSO, hardly surprising given where we place it on the competitive spectrum. A wide range of measures were both taken and used to improve performance. There was an understanding that more resources could be justified if they produced more business. However, there were still strains apparent between a culture of public accountability and one of pure commercialism. Delegated authority from Treasury to HMSO and downwards within HMSO was both expected and accepted (although it should be noted that our interviews here went no lower than the grade of SEO, fairly senior compared to the other Agencies). There was a general desire for even .more freedom from Treasury. Every manager interviewed was aware of the need to serve customers, both internal and external. A wide range of customer service measures were used regularly at the operational level and sometimes incorporated into the incentive structure (for industrial staff). The attitude towards restructuring (to four effective layers of management) was generally positive, although with a degree of nervousness about personal consequences. It was seen as likely to lead to greater flexibility to reward staff in relation to the commercial needs of the organization.

Again we are reminded that Agency status brought little change for this organization. As we concluded in Chapter 2, change would be more clearly perceived if any Agency's market or competitive stance were altered by Agency status. In our sample, it was not. Nor, for HMSO, was any increase in delegated authority noticed. One interviewee commented, 'Things have always been the same since I've been here: we have always been commercially minded, we have had ten years' practice.' In fact, because of their innovative restructuring proposals, there was a feeling that Treasury was taking a tighter overview. Another interviewee made a comment which was illustrative of the difficulty of operating in a politically constructed 'market' expressed to us by many managers: 'Sometimes the grade 7 managers are seen as more commercially aggressive than desired by their bosses or by ministers.'

Although many managers wanted more delegation from the centre, they appeared to have a reasonable degree already. In particular, budgets and performance measures were clearly linked to the needs of the business. Budgets were set in consultation: extra resources could be justified by extra business, while failure to meet targets could mean reducing resource costs. We were repeatedly told that moving money between budget heads was not a problem, it was the overall 'bottom line' which mattered.

At the Vehicle Inspectorate, which has previously benefited neither from commercial nor professional/scientific freedom, Agency status has had some impact on staff. This seems mostly at the level of increasing awareness of costs and customer service and of raising hopes for increased delegation within the Inspectorate. A number of current initiatives (like reorganization) are thought to derive from the 1982/3 privatization review, rather than from Agency status. As is so often the case with new initiatives, there is a time lag between promise and delivery. Staff hopes have been raised and yet little actual delegation appears to have taken place, which causes some frustration among staff. The Inspectorate appears to be strongly centrally managed. The Department of Transport and the Treasury are both seen as reluctant to judge by results, but instead to monitor closely and interfere. The Management Board is also perceived to involve itself too much in the day-to-day detail of running the organization, maybe because of the pressure faced by its members vis-à-vis the centre. Typical comments are, 'We would welcome the chance to choose between e.g. manpower and machines,' and, 'A line manager identifies a problem, the decision rests with the Chief Finance Officer.' The Management Board is seen to suffer from information overload, with information going up and down a chain of command and senior managers ordering action where necessary. There is a hint of the same approach with new business initiatives and customer service: a section is seen to be 'in charge' of these areas.

There is a general sense, however, that most staff approve of becoming an Agency and feel that their views are starting to be taken into consideration and that they can identify more closely with a smaller organization. As we say above, there may be a time lag effect: expectations raised before they can be fulfilled. Or perhaps the commercial or decentralized model simply does not fit so easily on a regulatory authority which spends taxpayers' money to fulfil statutory obligations. One interviewee said: 'fee structures are decided by the Department of Transport and the Treasury: this ought to be brought within the Agency'. There does not at present appear to be the will to achieve that level of decentralization.

At Warren Spring Laboratory, the move to Agency status was again generally perceived to have made little difference. An interviewee who joined the Laboratory about six months before it became an Agency commented: 'I have only been here two and a half years so I cannot honestly say that I have noticed a great deal of difference.' There is a feeling that having more control over personnel matters is an advantage. However, the majority feel that significant 'market' turbulence in recent years had had more impact on them than anything else. Significant policy changes, such as the 10% ceiling on direct industrial repayment work being lifted and then replaced and DTI ceasing to act as a proxy for industry and funding research are quoted as examples of environmental turbulence. Customer service measures are not widespread: the recurrent theme is that repeat business proves that customers are getting good service. However, there is also a sense that customers have to be led to understand what they want by Warren Spring experts — the recurrent dilemma of the professional supplier and the inexpert purchaser — and that sometimes staff have a good idea and then have to go out and find some customers who might be interested. Sometimes it appears to be the customer who decides if Warren Spring personnel can transfer between budgets, which is just the sort of difficulty we outlined above and might be expected when trying to separate purchasers and providers. Each knows too much about the other's detailed costs and procedures.

The evidence for this organization is mixed. At one level, a minority of respondents appear to have, or to take, budgetary responsibility. However, running projects for clients inevitably involves a degree of budgetary control. Certainly some staff want more budgetary involvement. There also appears to be a good understanding of new delegated personnel matters like promotion and local recruitment and Division Heads and the WSL Directorate are seen to be in charge of staffing levels.

Lastly, personnel at Companies House give a very positive impression of Agency status. Staff have a clear understanding both of the reasons for Agency status being sought and of the changes that being an Agency has brought. Staff also have ideas about what further delegations they would like. Budgetary responsibility had gone down as far as Executive Officer in some areas. There is a sense of a business-like organization, with involvement of staff right down the line in setting targets.

Performance measures are not collected for their own sake, nor for custodial purposes. There is an across-the-board awareness of customers, both internal and external, and of how quality of service delivery can be measured. This implies a concentration on monitoring outputs, or even outcomes, rather than inputs. New services have been adopted in addition to those made at the time of becoming an Agency, in response to customer requests. There is a sense of action, of line managers taking decisions and making things happen which previously would have engendered a lot of paperwork, or simply not have been undertaken at all. One HEO felt that he set staffing levels and commented that this is, 'one of the greatest benefits of Agency status'. Discussion of the changes is not limited to achieving targets: it also covers things like buying new furniture and having the central heating fixed, whereas 'no one had bothered before' because it had felt as if no one were in charge or responsible.

The picture here is positive, but not perfect. Old ways die hard as one quotation concerning annuality makes clear: 'Everyone is spending at the moment to avoid getting penalized next year.' Lack of training to underpin some of the changes seems to be the major issue: particularly difficult as the anticipated workload did not materialize during the first year of devolved budgets, so that cutbacks were necessary. Nonetheless, this Agency seems to have managed to decentralize markedly: evidence from our interviewees suggests that this is mainly due both to the former and the present Chief Executive of Companies House.

Department of Social Security

The DSS devolved expenditure control to lower levels but almost nothing else. This is reflected by the comments of one local office manager: 'When I first became a manager in 1982, I couldn't even buy a notice-board. Now we are given an overall staff budget and we have the authority to buy furniture and do our own repairs.'

One of the reasons for continuing centralization was that the department wants to achieve a reasonably uniform service level throughout the country, which implies that managers should be given very great operational freedom. Secondly, there is a nationally negotiated set of pay and conditions of employment and grades. It was not felt appropriate to give leeway to managers to change the pay rates (although this is now starting to happen in parts of the Civil Service). Managers can, however, vary the mix of grades in a local office according to local conditions. While local managers make bids for elements of the budget other than manpower, the staffing levels are set by manpower complements. Since staffing accounts for about 70% of the running cost budget, and many of the other running costs are fixed this implies a limited involvement by local managers in determining budgets. Meanwhile, the production function, product/service mix and distribution are almost entirely set by national policy.

However, even the small amounts of decentralization that the department has managed to achieve have been eroded by contraction in recent years, in other words, the department has been trying to run down the numbers of staff. One instrument in the management of contraction has been complementing, or the way that the department arrives at the number of staff required at each local office. The implications for budgetary control are profound because managers have found that you can run an office over complement and still stay within budget, yet the centre still requires local offices to reduce staff. One manager summed up the situation: 'It seems that we are running two schemes in parallel, those of staff *cost* and staff *numbers*. We are given the staff budget and then half way through the year we must reduce staff numbers. You then get the situation where you have spare cash but you can't spend it because you have to reduce the staff.'

With running costs, the system works slightly better although managers are still tied to certain suppliers but they have discretion, within limits, to use local contractors.

Apart from reducing staff numbers, another rationale for the complementing system is for the centre to ensure a national standard for local office delivery and so complementing is used as a mechanism to balance out staff numbers. The introduction of performance indicators has given the centre of the organization an impression that it exercises greater control. Since the establishment of the Benefits Agency in April 1991 the organization is committed to greater devolved management. District Managers have been appointed to run groups of about four Local Offices within the regional organization. Figure 4.3 illustrates the relationships prior to these changes.

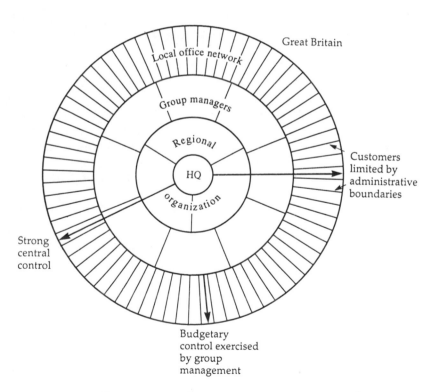

Figure 4.3   Department of Social Security (now Benefits Agency)

London Buses Ltd

There has been concern about London Transport's rising unit costs since the 1960s, together with their poor investment record and a deteriorating service. The organization was arranged functionally, with the functional divisions of 'traffic' and 'engineering' coming together only at the level of the Chairman of the London Transport Board. The momentum for a more devolved structure for LT, and for the bus operation in particular, developed as a result of questioning this centralized structure. Also: 'The rising share of total costs accounted for by engineering, and the need to improve availability at local level, has led to a more localized pattern.' (White, 1986).

A report by the Monopolies and Mergers Commission in 1980 highlighted the need for a localized pattern which subsequently began to emerge.

One result was the establishment of eight bus districts although one director saw this as a result of a political impetus which: '... came from the Conservative government as the subsidy began to escalate, LT was no longer value for money. However, the progressive reduction of subsidy outstripped quality of service and this became part of the reason for setting up the districts' (interview with director).

Another reason for the setting up of the districts was: '... to clarify lines of management and financial control, and delegate more decision-making to local management with a fuller knowledge of conditions in their areas'. (Garbutt, 1985).

The next important change was the enactment of the London Regional Transport Act 1984. Many non-executive members on the former LT executive had been placed there by the GLC and these were replaced by members from the private sector on the new LRT board; the style of management at the top changed overnight.

Another important requirement of the Act was the obligation to invite tenders: 'London Regional Transport shall ... invite other persons to submit tenders to carry on those activities for such period and on such basis as may be specified in the invitation to tender.' (para 6 (1)).

Tendering would help to keep down unit costs, and indeed they were to come down by about 20% in the following five years. It also introduced competition to public transport in London for the first time. 'Tendering ... was a tremendous spur to productivity. It helped to free up a lot of working practices and reduce the total cost of labour.' (LBL Board Member). There was also agreement that it forced managers to make their own decisions in order to respond to the market and the customer. No public revenue is used for tendering for routes in competition with the private sector as LRT would continue to receive a block grant from the government.

The Act heralded the start of a difficult process for management but many of those to whom we spoke felt that the Act was the major impetus to decentralization in LBL. Further impetus came from the appointment of John Telford Beasley in 1984 as Chief Executive of LRT and Chair of LBL and, as one board member observed: 'he sees the best way of serving customers as being on a local basis with local managers'.

Further pressure for change came from Nicholas Ridley, then Secretary of State for Transport, who demanded from LRT proposals for the establishment of separate subsidies for the buses and Underground. He also called for a devolution of the bus subsidy to smaller units that would match supply and demand and more vigorous strides towards competitive tendering. LBL is now being prepared for eventual deregulation followed by privatization. Further deregulation of London Buses was announced with the Citizen's Charter in July 1991. Aucoin (1990) notes that along with decentralization, ideas about deregulation of the public sector are gaining prominence: 'The logic of deregulation rests on the assumption that line managers are best positioned to secure efficiency, economy and effectiveness in public management and that, freed from the obstacles of regulations, they will produce results.'

While the devolution to the companies and the garages implied decentralized financial control, all major decisions on product/service mix, production function and distribution remained with LRT. All government support is distributed through LRT who also determine fares, routes, control property and own the buses. Because LRT control the subsidies and fare structure, budget making at company level is restricted to constructing bids and budgetary discretion is limited. LBL has been unable to give the companies complete freedom because they are still publicly subsidized.

In LBL, one garage general manager (GGM) talked of staff needing to be 're-educated'. This was because there was an important distinction to be made: 'The difference is between customer orientation and service orientation. We should realize that the customers will be soon paying our wages so everyone needs to see the job as an income producer.'

This represents a fundamental shift that can be applied to the whole of the public sector: managers are now regarding their businesses as income generators rather than processes of allocating resources. One GGM kept asking himself the question: are we meeting existing demand? He felt that this question was an increasingly important part of his job. He also regarded market evaluation as equally important, yet he still felt that he was generating the information for LRT and not his company.

Decentralization in LBL also meant considerable management restructuring, with the 'centre' (LBL HQ) shrinking as the newly established subsidiary companies absorbed functions previously dealt with at HQ.

Therefore, LBL had to be sure that the newly appointed company Managing Directors could cope with the demands that would be placed on them. A senior director told us that: 'When selecting the managing directors, we were looking for entrepreneurs within a nationalized industry, if they can't accept this, they will have to go elsewhere but I accept the two do not sit happily together. It is possible to let the entrepreneurial side come out with tendering and they do know that they have to wait for deregulation and 'privatization . . .'.

It is agreed that tendering has sharpened management thinking from a situation where 'individual enterprise was not expected or rewarded' and managers simply implemented policy. However, many long-serving managers could not make the change. GGMs have also appreciated the new environment in which they can change and learn new skills, although a tension still remains: 'The dilemma is that we are being encouraged to think commercially yet we are still required to behave as a public service because we receive the block grant. LRT acts on behalf of London and decides on the mileage to be run for social reasons.'

Many of the new jobs, especially the managing directors, were advertised externally but there were difficulties in getting the right people to come and work in London. However, many former HQ staff have joined the companies which helped to shrink the 'centre'.

The new company management structure was seen as the 'last centrally imposed solution'. Part of the reorganization was the elimination of supervisory grades that diluted responsibilities. These have been replaced by assistant operations and engineering managers and clerical support. The new posts of Operations and Engineering Managers are seen as 'a good thing' now that they have a focus of responsibility. It was hoped that a different attitude would be held to the new jobs that were created: 'we had to change the culture at all levels'.

The creation of Garage General Managers was an innovatory step for LBL as well as an attempt to help engender a better working relationship between staff and management. Motivation is helped by the GGM being able to reward long service and good performance. The success of this innovation will be reflected in the GGMs' own statistics for sickness leave and staffing levels, but there is still the frustration that underspends cannot be used to reward staff for productivity. Also, 'it was not productive in the old days to have managers sat behind desks dishing out discipline'. Now, it is claimed that discipline has improved since the GGMs were given authority over hiring and firing. Company directors concede that they are now removed from 'sharp-end decision making', which has gone to the GGMs.

One GGM sums up the impact of decentralization on his job: 'The extent to which my work has changed is shown by the fact that I am required to adopt a more thinking and conceptualized aspect rather than working within a job description.'

Company directors are actively trying to create a small company atmosphere as well as forging local identities: each company has its own logo. This has resulted in conflict between LBL and LRT because unity is still required over, say, the colour of the buses. On the one hand, managers are told to act commercially but on the other, house rules continue to be imposed by LRT. However, LBL has helped the companies to challenge LRT traditions. One MD commented that: 'We are hampered by a rigid design philosophy but I am working towards brand loyalty if we want customer loyalty. We have to carve out our own niche of the market and be ready for deregulation.'

Pay bargaining has now been decentralized to the companies and the directors will be able to qualify for performance bonuses in the form of increments provided they meet certain criteria, some of which is quantitative (mileage, engineering performance etc.) and some of which is qualitative (dealing with public correspondence etc.). There will be a direct link between the managing directors and the performance of the company.

One MD saw the real challenge as being for the staff in the garages to realize that the buses are now in a commercial world and that the staff will want to go with the companies. The serious threat of competition had sharpened thinking in LBL about the jobs that people actually do, hence the creation of new posts and the dissolution of others, resulting in a considerable cultural change.

However, not only is the LBL HQ in Victoria contracting, but personnel managers at the company level too, for instance, will see their roles diminishing. One company director commented: 'My line responsibilities have been limited to a vestigial personnel function that is shrinking as the garages take over more recruitment and training.'

LBL is still evolving, and full decentralization will have to be achieved before the subsidiary bus companies start to compete with each other when LBL is privatized. This all depends on the political will of central government. The current arrangements are illustrated in Figure 4.4.

Impact on the service deliverers

It is reasonable to expect that the reforms public sector organizations have experienced will have a great impact on those that deliver the services, the 'front-line' staff. If decentralizing an organization, or opening it up to competition, or both, involves allowing greater freedom of action for the

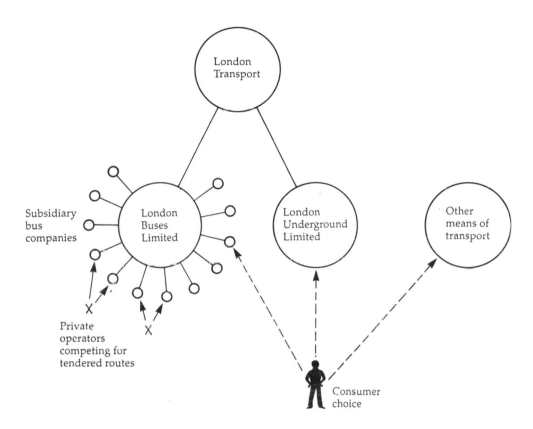

Figure 4.4   London Buses Ltd

staff as well as more involvement in decision making, then a considerable cultural change is likely to occur within the organization.

The impact of the reforms on the managers should generally have a similar effect. One difficulty here is whether to attribute managerial changes of behaviour to more general reforms affecting the organizations concerned or to actual initiatives that increase competition or promote decentralization. For instance, respondents in the Executive Agencies often had difficulty in ascribing change to agency status. There are, of course, the managers who have found themselves with new freedoms and responsibilities, but there are also those who have become more frustrated because change has been slow or practice has differed from the theory. There are some who think the changes have made no difference at all to the way they work. Yet pay determination, working practices, and attitudes are slowly beginning to change. The impact of training is often underestimated. Staff frequently complain of being 'thrown in at the deep end', yet a perceived lack of support could be alleviated by training.

Decentralization has brought new pressures for managers: meeting and setting targets; compiling statistics; personnel management; financial management; measuring and assessing service delivery; and marketing. Managers are *having* to behave differently. If the main aim of decentralization is to improve public services, we can expect the style of public service delivery to alter.

Conclusions

What does this experience tell us about the desirable or likely degree of autonomy for local managers in the public sector?

First, the motivation for decentralization is an important determinant of the real degree of autonomy for managers. If the real reason for delegation is to save money by sharpening accountability, it is likely that managers will be held accountable for spending and may be asked to construct their own budgets.

If real efficiency savings are desired, this should involve a change in the way in which products and services are made and delivered. This may represent too much risk for an organization which does not believe in the capabilities of its managers. If the managers are treated as administrators of a system of production and delivery which has been pre-designed elsewhere, it is unlikely that they will be given any real discretion over the input mix or the service process. This creates real tension if managers at lower levels are led to believe that they are being treated more seriously as managers.

If the motivation for the decentralization is to create more responsive services and to tailor them more closely to local needs, then local managers need to be given a high degree of autonomy over the way services are produced. Other steps can be taken to increase the likelihood of this happening. For example, at London Buses Ltd, the managing directors of the new subsidiaries were recruited from outside so that they would more readily accept, or demand, a higher degree of autonomy than incumbent managers. This is also a growing trend in Executive Agencies: for example, the second Chief Executive at Companies House, Mr David Durham, has a public sector background but is not of the central Civil Service, Whitehall culture.

Thus it seems that the *motivation* for restructuring will affect the amount of decentralization actually permitted. Moreover, it appears that decentralization or restructuring is not sufficient on its own. There needs to be the will to use the freedoms gained to *make* managerial life seem different.

Companies House Executive Agency is a good example here. They do not face real competition, but managers feel as if they do. They have had two Chief Executives. The first, Stephen Curtis, was very keen on using all the delegations gained: a very early, symbolic (but very necessary) act was to take on 100 temporary clerical staff within three weeks, an unheard-of achievement under a system of central recruitment. The current Chief Executive, David Durham, has been described by his staff as 'dedicated to delegation'. Staff down to and in some cases including clerical staff are involved in setting and monitoring budgets. We return to these ideas in Chapter 7.

Change is happening at all levels in the organizations we studied, yet seems to be felt least by those who are furthest down the hierarchy. A frequent comment from this group was that the only perceived change was a greater focus on tighter targets and performance measures. So at best, interviewees said that the changes had not affected the way they do their jobs; at worst, they said the only thing they had become conscious of was increasing pressure of work-loads. Organizations which have been through a process of decentralization place new demands on all the staff, not just those at the centre. Concern and anxiety on the part of the staff are understandable responses.

Some of this confusion can be relieved by being clear about the purpose of decentralization: it has to be thoroughly managed. So the first requirement is that there should be no ambiguity about the purpose of the exercise: if increased control over expenditure is the real underlying agenda of senior management, rhetoric about increased flexibility will probably produce cynicism among middle managers and staff. If the real reason is to enable local managers to be more responsive to their customers or users, then the rules and procedures must also be aligned with that aim. Nominal delegation, for example expressed through new job descriptions, will not increase responsiveness without accompanying improved access to resource control.

Once the reasons for the change have been clarified and a new set of rules, procedures and freedoms have been agreed, the message must be spread throughout the organization. Our research has shown that it is possible for the crucial people, the front-line workers, to be unaware of changes which senior management thought had been implemented. Successful decentralization empowers people in an unmistakable way.

If people are to take on new tasks and responsibilities they will almost certainly require training and development. The Benefits Agency has further decentralized much of its managerial control in its Regional Organization to local and group management level, starting from the launch of the Agency in April 1991, continuing the process reported earlier in this chapter. The change was accompanied by a training effort in many of the skill areas required by the managers, such as investment appraisal and customer service. Without training, people will not have the confidence to take on new responsibilities.

In the next chapter we discuss the impact of managerial changes on the customers or users. Decentralization only allows a customer to gain more power if the local workers and managers themselves have discretion over service delivery and some control over resources. Even then, there is no *necessary* increase in user power: they may exchange the tyranny of the centralized bureaucracy for the petty autocracy of the local manager. Good feedback from users, systematic measurement of performance and a shared understanding of user's entitlements are all necessary elements of getting 'close to the customer' in the public sector.

5 The impact on the customer

Introduction

'Although the customer is not always right, we now have a different attitude to supplying a reasonable service' (manager in an Executive Agency).

In the previous chapter we saw that there are many motivations for decentralization. Only one was about making the organizations 'closer to the customer' in the sense of being able to listen to the service users and respond to what they are saying. This objective may exist from the government's point of view only at the level of rhetoric: the objectives about increasing accountability and further controlling costs may have been the dominant motive with the idea of responsiveness used as an afterthought.

However, providing a good service is an important motivator for managers, professionals and other workers. Many define a good service in relation to what the service users or customers want. In this sense the pursuit of customer service is a rather different 'lever' than competition or decentralization in the sense that it may be a lever which is developed by the managers themselves, rather than being imposed from outside.

The quest for good customer service may be used as a surrogate for real competition as a spur to good management: often, public sector service providers remain monopolies. But they can use the same methods of improving service as they would if they were using these methods to lure customers away from some other service provider.

In competitive situations it is relatively easy to see whether an organization has been successful in attracting customers: monopolies have to see whether or not their monopoly customers are satisfied. While there is no imperative to measure success, many monopolies decide to test the reaction to their services. This enhances the accountability of the services to their users but may cut across accountability to democratic institutions (local authorities or Parliament). This can be a real problem for managers. Elected members of local authorities feel that their function as the conduit of opinions and preferences from the electorate to the managers is undermined by consumer surveys. Ministers are often reluctant to release the results of consumer surveys because they may contradict their own, optimistic messages about the quality of services.

Because of this difficulty, developing a customer orientation can be dangerous for managers; their other stakeholders, the politicians, may have a vested interest in a lack of communication: finding out what users think, what they prefer and how satisfied or dissatisfied they are may be an important step in the empowerment of the service users. If this power implies that more money should be spent on the services or that standards should be improved it could be part of the campaign for more resources to be allocated to whatever service is concerned. Politicians or the Treasury may prefer not to know. One senior manager in the former Department of Social Security told us: 'When considering the question of an agency being more responsive to its customers, we cannot consider a private sector model. The customers in this case can only exercise leverage through the policy process, thus attacking the idea that agencies will insulate managers. This aspect is recognized by the department as politics will provide the surrogate for the market.'

On the other hand if service users are treated as 'customers' and their satisfaction or dissatisfaction can be interpreted as being a result of the strength or otherwise of the managers' abilities to deliver this can reduce the accountability of politicians. Some of the elements of the Citizen's Charter can achieve this end. For example if passengers are compensated by British Rail for the delayed arrival of trains, it implies that British Rail and its managers are at fault. If the underlying reason for delays is a history of underinvestment in signalling equipment and rolling stock or of staff shortages, this will not be apparent to the passenger in the role of 'customer'. In the role of citizen, the rail user could rightly complain of the government's policy towards transport in general and the funding of the railway in particular. As customers they can only blame management.

Our third criterion for measuring the success of the managerial changes was whether they made any impact on the users or 'customers' of the services. Internal change and restructuring keeps people busy but does it make any real difference?

This chapter looks at the extent to which the organizations studied monitored the impact of competition, decentralization and customer focus on the users of public services. It then goes on to explore some of the issues in public sector market research. Implicit in these reforms is changing the relationship between the service provider and service user, but changing this relationship uncovers special problems in the public sector, such as the difficulty of serving someone when you also regulate by statute. How can we measure successful improvement in the service given to customers?

One measure that consumers might use is the amount of choice they are offered. However, the inherent problem with public services is that in many cases, no real choice can be offered due to statutory requirements and administrative boundaries. Therefore, there has been no real imperative, or indeed, little need, to devote resources to finding out what customers really want. One important aspect of the current changes is that more attention is being given to the needs and preferences of customers.

In order to gauge the impact of the reforms on users, or indeed to find out what users really want you have to ask them. However, market research is still in its infancy in the public sector and very often surveys that have been carried out tend to cover general levels of satisfaction and avoid assessing the impact of changes, managerial or otherwise, on customers. The idea of introducing market research into the public sector is not new. For instance, in 1970, Tony Benn, at the Conference of the Market Research Society, called for the application of market research techniques to social and welfare problems. However, making proper assessments of customer satisfaction and preferences has been traditionally low on the agenda of public sector managers. Simply responding to complaints often served the function of raising the awareness of managers when services were being poorly provided. Often, organizations would have inadequate channels through which complaints could be made, and positive opinions were unlikely to be sought. Many organizations used the level of complaints as a criterion for success: if they received no complaints, the service was judged to be satisfactory.

Even if threatened with competition, public sector organizations are inevitably constrained by available resources and finance from engaging in a meaningful evaluation of service effectiveness but they can look at ways in which the consumer can evaluate and ask questions about the service provided for them. The public sector organizations under scrutiny are aware of the importance of a strategy that looks at the needs and satisfactions of users or customers. For instance, the success of executive agencies will be partly judged on customer satisfaction. Writing about the NHS, Sir Roy Griffiths saw it as the duty of senior management to: 'ascertain how well the service is being delivered at the local level by obtaining the experience and perceptions of patients and the community: these can be derived from Community Health Councils and other methods, including market research'.

Although there is an awareness of the needs of the customer and there are attempts to respond to those needs, managers continue to be constrained by statutory frameworks, lack of resources and sometimes a professional culture which can see the service user simply as a cog in the service delivery cycle. External constraints like legislation mean that often the debate is held at the level of how well current services are delivered, rather than considering new services. However, user involvement in a variety of ways, from passenger surveys on buses to parent–governors of schools, is now on the agenda of senior management. Also, selling becomes a more important activity when in competition. So, for example, schools now see the need to market themselves and assess the potential market beyond traditional catchment areas. The subsidiary companies of London Buses Limited have marketing functions with an eye to likely competition with each other in the near future.

1   Northamptonshire Police

The Police and Criminal Evidence Act of 1984 helped encourage the notion of the consumer in the police service. This was achieved by requiring each police force to obtain the views of local people regarding police matters and for them to be able to work with the police in crime prevention. Two examples to grow from this are community consultative groups and 'lay visitor' schemes for police stations.

Northamptonshire Police, although not in competition with other police authorities, is attempting to become more responsive to its customers. It has tried to go beyond community consultative groups in involving the public. Northamptonshire police see their 'customers' as all those members of the public who actually come into contact with the force, whether it is to report a crime or actually being arrested.

Another way of making the force more responsive was by decentralizing aspects of inspection. Decentralization allowed customer service to be developed in the subdivisions under the umbrella of 'self-inspection' programmes which were initiated by a subdivision commander to encourage middle managers (inspectors and sergeants) to accept responsibility for good service. One significant feature of self-inspection is regular customer sampling during which: 'customer satisfaction' is 'tested in a scientific manner: there is a random 10% check across the subdivision and' it is hoped 'to get a fair assessment of how the customer feels'.

Quality checking is therefore used to establish the level of service given to the public. Each officer is expected to make contact with twelve customers (anyone who comes into contact with the subdivision) in a 28-day cycle and work through a standard questionnaire. The questions deal with both quantitative and qualitative issues as well as an attempt to gauge public opinions about the service in general in the section 'Policing in Your Area'. What happens after the information is gathered can affect the way that the subdivision delivers the service, and how Northamptonshire Police concentrates resources through the PBO cycle.

As part of the inspection process, divisional commanders then examine the quality of service delivered by the subdivisions. Part of the process is looking at how they are using and deploying resources and how they respond to calls from the public. There are no formal performance measurements but a concern over meeting 'professional' standards. Policing by objectives is a way of giving priority to the types of crime 'that lead to the greatest public fear of crime'. This means making decisions where resources are channelled and evaluating these decisions after listening to the public.

The officers we interviewed thought that service to the public had improved immeasurably since the adoption of PBO and that management had become more 'professional' as a result. For instance, PBO helped subdivisions establish Beat Crime Units to leave CID to concentrate on more serious crimes, which has helped some subdivisions become more efficient in clearing cases. However, one difficulty is that police performance is related to crime statistics and despite public attitude surveys being conducted, it is usually the numbers which take precedence in the end. Northamptonshire Police are trying to move away from this; in the words of a Chief Inspector: ' "Policing by objectives" is about demonstrating effectiveness but it doesn't mean that you ignore other issues. Measurement is difficult although we are moving away from a reliance on statistics to a more qualitative assessment. We measure public satisfaction by survey and the level of complaints as well as constant internal monitoring.'

2   Kent Local Education Authority

In 1987, Kent County Council commissioned MORI to undertake a research study on public attitudes to council services, including education. Questions about choice of schools came under the heading of 'Reasons for Dissatisfaction with Schools'. For primary schools, 'no choice of schools' was mentioned by only a small percentage of respondents as a reason for dissatisfaction. The figure was slightly higher for secondary schools but here the 'limited choice' reason was grouped with 'school closures'. 'Choice of school' was also way down the list headed by 'lack of funding for materials and equipment' for primary schools and 'lack of discipline' for secondary schools.

Schools in Kent seemed to hold the general view that they had been in competition since the 1980 Education Act. However, this did vary. For instance, one headteacher felt that competition should not inhibit the school's main duty, which is to provide a good broad education. Another headteacher did not regard his school as in competition because of the absence of alternatives in the area. The school was a local monopoly. The advent of formula funding is likely to sharpen competition when the schools who are more judicious in the management of money are able to divert resources to marketing. Schools saw that a competitive edge could be gained through marketing and 'flagships'. A flagship, in this instance, refers to alternative uses of school property. They were special projects that raised the profile of the school as well as generating income such as bookshops and IT suites. However, there was common concern among headteachers that difficult pupils might undermine marketing strategies.

Kent also aimed to expand its market research to include qualitative work which involved paying attention to less obvious issues. For instance, it was considered that the Education committee reports that were published were not 'user friendly' so some work was done with the Plain English campaign: they believed that improving this type of communication was crucial to an overall consumer orientation. Therefore, the LEA recognized the need for a strong information system which advises families of alternatives along with a transportation system to make school choices accessible (see Levin, 1989)

3   London Buses Limited

Before the 1960s, there seemed to be plenty of passengers and little competition. Public transport did not especially feel the need to be responsive to its users. In the case of London Buses, one reason why managers may have lacked a consumer orientation in the past was because they have been subject to evaluation on cost-based criteria rather than on revenue criteria. Lovelock *et al.* (1987) said: 'When operations are in a cost-centred environment, managers and staff are likely to be driven inward to focus on their operation rather than outward to reach toward their customers.' They proposed the decentralization of revenue responsibility as one solution to this problem: revenue generated is a good indicator of how valuable the bus service is to its customers. However, this is unlikely to occur in London Buses because revenue collection from buses, underground and railways is coordinated by London Transport. Also, the prevalence of travel cards covering all public transport obscures bus revenue as only a small proportion of revenue is generated 'on bus'. Although it is possible to identify points of revenue generation, for instance, at the local underground station, this is complicated by the fact that travelcards etc. are available at newsagents. One commercial director expands on this problem: 'Are we getting the right deal from the split of travel-card revenue on a garage basis? It constitutes 60% of our income and proportions are still determined centrally. One example of this problem is that although travel cards induce people to the suburban rail-heads, we have no incentive to increase the number of buses to get them there. The apportionment has to be right at the margins. Data collection is still difficult and is indicative of the problems still faced.'

However despite these difficulties London Buses have attempted to make their organization more responsive. Before decentralization, London Buses were covered by London Regional Transport's Marketing function. This began to be gradually devolved to LBL when it was established in 1985. John Telford-Beesley, appointed as Chair of the buses division in 1984, reinforced the ideas of marketing and customer care in the organization and believed that the best way of serving customers was on a local basis with local managers. This involved a considerable cultural change for London Buses but with little accompanying competitive stimulus.

It is widely believed in LBL that service to the customer has improved with decentralization; for instance, one manager commented that now the buses are reducing costs without worsening the service to the public, something that was deemed impossible with the former centralized organization. Furthermore, decentralization, to some extent, has helped to empower local managers to act in the interests of their customers. For example, the U-Line service in Uxbridge was initiated by a Garage Operations manager who then acted as a project manager. However, his report had to be approved by LBL and then by LRT. Having been given permission to proceed, he then organized the purchase of the buses, negotiated with local residents and handled staff recruitment and pay deals. A company director commented that: 'This was a huge responsibility for a manager and it would not have been possible a short time ago.'

Another move has been to make managers responsible for bus routes, and their names have been put on the buses. This is all part of an effort to introduce accountability into the organization.

London Buses see their main indicator of customer satisfaction as letters from customers and now the public can write directly to garage general managers rather than the headquarters. Therefore, correspondence that used to take two to three weeks to deal with can now be dealt with immediately.

There was a general view among LBL managers that the quality of service had improved, reflected by the improvement in performance indicators such as mileage, percentage of vehicles turning up for service and the presentation of vehicles. One GGM summed up why he thought decentralization had been useful in helping LBL respond to the customer: By the end of next year (1990), we should be able to set our services to what the customer demands and I can take my own initiatives for customer care.'

4 Executive Agencies

Executive Agencies are designed, among other things, to improve service to the customer. Formal targets were set with this in mind. For example, Companies House was required to reduce by 20% the time taken to process documents, so that by April 1991, the average time taken between accounts being submitted and made available to the public was 18 working days. For HMSO, the targets were more comprehensive, including 100% of print orders to be delivered without fault. National Weights and Measures Laboratory (NWML) divided its targets into output, effectiveness and efficiency measures, which are all essentially quantitative. The same quantitative approach applied to the Vehicle Inspectorate. Only Warren Spring Laboratory (WSL) had a target based on outcomes: 'The primary performance measure is the Agency's ability to win and maintain custom in a competitive situation, so that it fully recovers its costs from customers.'

The kind of performance indicators being established in the agencies are often concerned with improving the current service rather than diversification into new services. However, Agency status has allowed some managers to innovate in accordance to their customer's demands. At Companies House, for instance, new services have been introduced in addition to those changes made at the time of becoming an Agency, in response to customer's requests. There is also a Customer Care team so that larger clients have a named contact within the organization.

At WSL, there was the view that the best (and only) measure of customer service is customers coming back. But apart from repeat business, other methods used to gauge customer satisfaction fall into two categories: checking that contract specifications are met, and customer feedback. The approach varies from individual to individual rather than being driven by any policy. For example, one officer took a more proactive approach and had commissioned an attitude survey among customers and had made changes to the service as a result of this. The same individual also met customers at least once a year to listen to suggestions. Another respondent was interested in the idea of a customer survey, but mentioned that WSL was resource constrained. Another mentioned that, because of the limit set on work done for industry (10%), if approached by a large industrial customer, the customer might actually have to be turned away.

NWML is a tiny Agency, employing only 50 staff. Perhaps necessarily then, the general approach is that new services might be offered if requested and the current workload permitted it. Certainly no attempt was made to sell its services and in fact managers encouraged other suppliers. Again the classic difficulty of having two sets of customers with conflicting aims, in this case Trading Standard's officers and manufacturers, was highlighted. There had been no customer surveys but they had undertaken a customer consultation exercise in which a joint committee of NWML staff and established customers reviewed the pattern examination procedures. As a result, several changes were made to administrative and technical aspects of the service.

Staff at Companies House (CH) understand that service to internal customers is just as important in order to enable improved service to external customers. Staff gather information about customer service by questionnaire, by meeting customers and by using a professional market research company, Indal, who carried out some initial research and supplement this with six-monthly updates. New initiatives have been introduced or are being considered, in addition to the ones which were introduced when CH became an agency. For example, a same-day service for company registration is being considered. New services include longer opening hours, two-hour search targets for everyone and the Value Added Network, where customers can access the CH database remotely and order searches.

Opinion varies about the origin of approval for new initiatives, but it definitely feels as if responsibility has been decentralized, so that approval is perceived to come from the Steering Board or from within CH rather than from DTI. People talk about making a 'business case'; of the customer not always being right, but of taking a different attitude to supplying a reasonable service; and of those who must comply with legislation and submit their accounts as being customers, who should have their information put onto fiche as soon as possible.

At the Vehicle Inspectorate (VI), ideas about customer service are not universal: some were unsure who their customers might be. However, there is increasing use of market research and of negotiation with customers, for instance, informal service agreements. Service providers are trying to develop new measures rather than relying on complaints. Some new services are being suggested (e.g. selling minor spares) and some enacted (e.g. local test bookings). The success of new services is generally measured by take-up.

The situation was different at HMSO where there was a clear 'business culture'. This was reflected in attitudes among managers about service to the customer both internal and external: targets are used to measure both. Changes to services are made at the operational level, to meet changed customer needs, although more changes are referred to Board level. There is the power to offer a 'loss leader' to attract new custom. Two customer surveys were mentioned and managers invited customers to come and discuss their requirements.

The Department of Social Security has used professional market research to find out what claimants think are the most important elements of service and how satisfied they are. The results have enabled managers to concentrate on those elements, such as privacy and confidentiality, which the claimants feel are important. More extensive local use of market research is developing since the launch of the Executive Agency.

Using market research in the public sector

Market research is vital if we are to gauge properly the impact of the reforms on the users of public services. Kieron Walsh (1991), writing about the importance of marketing to local government, argued that: 'Detailed market information is necessary if the organization is to be able to make specific decisions and monitor their impact.'

Some public sector organizations have been taking their own market research initiatives for a number of years. For example, Cleveland County Council has conducted an annual survey since 1975 covering a broad range of issues. The researchers discovered that marketing services were a problem, given that usually only one-fifth of respondents felt that they were being adequately informed. They also suggested that such surveys often reveal unfavourable findings so far as the local authority is concerned, thus offering part of the explanation as to why so few local authorities bother to use them at all.

Furze (1986) analysed market research activity in local authorities undertaking decentralization initiatives. The London Borough of Camden in 1983, before embarking on a programme of decentralization, surveyed residents about their opinions. For example, respondents were asked to say how much they agreed or disagreed with the statement, 'the borough of Camden is too big and should be split into smaller units'. When preparing organizational change or changes to service delivery market research can prevent problems arising after implementation, especially when these services are complex. For instance, Young and Hadley (1990) point to East Sussex social services department who used 'systematic surveys of user opinion' that not only helped in the evaluation of the work of the department but whose results were also made available to those who had taken part, encouraging user involvement.

However, Furze concluded that: 'The science of opinion-surveying in local government is still only weakly developed but experience is growing fast.'

Chisnall (1986) quotes a leading market researcher who remarked that public sector organizations have been slow to use market research because they are often monopoly suppliers. If this is the case, there is the danger that without proper research, judgements left to policy makers or professionals may be ill-advised. This view is echoed by Cartwright (1983) when writing about the health service: 'the most fundamental contribution made by surveys in the health field is that most of them are concerned with the needs, experiences and attitudes of patients in a service which might otherwise be dominated by professional paternalism'.

If public sector organizations are serious about responding to their users and conducting consumer research, what sort of questions should they be asking? If questions are being asked about the consumer's preferences, then this presupposes the consumer has a choice. If the reforms in the public sector are about giving choice to the user, then what do we mean by choice? For the user, there are two basic choices: which type of service to use, and which supplier to use. Survey data should be used to help maximize the choice available to consumers.

In the public sector, choice will be inevitably restricted by available finance, resources or legislation, but wherever possible, choice should be widened within these constraints. This may require innovative approaches for successful implementation. If we use the example of community care, the following questions are likely to be raised: how much choice of day care will an elderly person have? Will they be restricted to a particular price bracket or geographical area? How far will the case manager go in restricting the choice? Having established the entitlement will the choice be left completely open for the client and their family (Flynn and Common, 1990). Consumer research needs to ask questions about choice in core and peripheral services and also about the possibility of new services.

As we have seen, the culture of public sector organizations is changing to the extent that all those involved in the delivery of public services are getting used to the idea of customer service, be it the public they are serving or colleagues using their services within the organization (the internal market). Many difficulties are raised in the conduct of consumer research and many of them come from not asking the right questions. For instance, MORI, on behalf of the London Borough of Richmond, asked the public in its 1990 survey about setting up two local offices to deal with Housing, Finance and Social Services, the questions were:

'Please can you tell me if, in principle, you favour or oppose the setting up of local offices?'
and
'If a local council office is set up in this area, which, if any, of these types of location do you consider would be best?'

The first question offers two extremes and does not elicit the consumer's needs. The second talks about types of location rather than locations: choice is immediately limited. The council will have information on opposition or otherwise to its local offices and what kind of buildings people want to put them in but choice and access do not come into the picture.

Christopher Bowles of the Greater Manchester Passenger Transport Executive recognized that market research was an important part of the 'marketing mix' for public transport. 'The Executive's prime corporate objective is to maximize its patronage and to limit any decline to that resulting from external factors. To meet that objective and to measure results needs a thorough market research organization.'

Greater Manchester Transport employed a full-time survey team following two methods: continuous passenger sampling and specific service sampling. They also used market research agencies to assess consumer opinion on matters such as fares policies, quality of service, publicity and information (Bowles, 1983).

In education, the introduction of local management of schools (LMS) and 'opting out' is seen as a market approach that will be more responsive to consumers in the sense that it will provide more options. Where there is no competition between schools, market surveys can be used to establish what families want from their local monopoly supplier, consumers' experience and the acceptability of the current service.

HMSO commissioned a research project in 1990 to try to find out their customers' views. The stated objective was to maintain and then stimulate new custom. The overall conclusion of the research was that HMSO had succeeded in becoming more customer orientated, especially in its efforts to become more flexible: using the customer's order form instead of HMSO's was one example. It is interesting to note that qualitative interviews were used as the research method: the research side-stepped quantitative methods.

In health, Luck *et al.* (1988) saw the fundamental aim of surveys about the acceptability of services as being to use the results to plan services to take account of 'patients' experiences and preferences' as well as simply using it to assess satisfaction with current services. However, this is difficult when respondents have experienced no alternatives.

The NHS commissioned MORI in 1989 to survey consumers of the NHS. Questions covered use of health services; choice of services; waiting times and appointments; and access to services. The results were compared with a previous survey carried out in 1979–80. A second block of questions attempted to elucidate consumer's attitudes to 'Working for Patients'. Questions then covered choice of hospital; GP budgets; self-governing hospitals and prescribing by GPs. But does this kind of survey really measure the impact of health service reforms? Although use of the health service has changed little in the comparative analysis, scant attention is paid to choice: 'Few people in 1989 reported difficulties with choice of health services. The only significant figure was the five per cent of those who had used a hospital casualty department or attended hospital as an in-patient who said that they had experienced some problems over choice.'

This represents the common dilemma of the public sector: when does need become choice? Can you offer choice to someone who has just had a serious accident? The patient is unlikely to choose a more distant hospital casualty department just because he had received a brochure from them the previous day. This also raises the question about access to services: if you cannot get access to the service you want, then there is no choice. However, the MORI survey reported a 'high degree of satisfaction' with access to services. Is this likely to change if hospitals speciailize and what are the implications for those who cannot travel or cannot afford to travel?

When asking consumers for their opinions about 'Working for Patients', the question was: 'how important would it be that you and your GP should be able to choose which hospital you should attend?' Implicit in the question was the assumption that the GP would not only act as purchasing agent for those in his or her care but it is the GP who would have the information that would influence choice. It is also interesting to note that when MORI asked consumers whom they thought should be consulted before a hospital became a self-governing trust, the group 'doctors and nurses at the hospital' came out on top. The research confirmed that the reforms are not consumer-led at all.

Also, the management reforms of the 1980s in the NHS had done little to sensitize managers to the needs of their consumers. Pollitt *et al.* (1988) concluded that, 'the development of greater consumer responsiveness is not an issue which emerged well from our research'. Overall, it was felt that little consumer orientation was occurring, and when it did, it was greeted with cynicism. For managers, finance was the priority issue.

Furthermore, in the NHS, although service mix and delivery show variations between different health districts, this variation is not linked to consumer need. Harrison (1989) claimed that there has always been competition in the health service, especially in urban areas and when considering the number of patients admitted to the London teaching hospitals. However, variations between authorities are based on how services have been developed and delivered in the past. Detailed consumer research would therefore help to assess the real health care needs of the local population. Keleher and Cole (1989) propose the following steps in empowering the NHS consumer:

- Increased involvement of consumers in planning and evaluating services.
- The development of a positive attitude to consumer research of health districts to identify real health related needs, attitudes and behaviours.

● Increased liaison with the local authority (social services and education) as well as voluntary or charity groups. Often local groups will have useful information on consumer behaviour for certain segments.
● Links with local industry and commerce could be better forged.

If, as in the case of the NHS, choice continues to lie in the hands of providers, then one consumer research strategy may be to ask consumers to base their judgements of a service on professional criteria such as those used by HMI or local authority social services departments and adapting these into a checklist. Care would need to be taken in giving advance notice to users and customers of what they were being asked to do and clarity required about how the information was to be used.

Care would also need to be taken over the scope of such a survey. If the reforms in the public sector are about decentralization and competition, there may be problems with approaching consumers and users over agencies such as a district health authority, a local education authority, LRT or whatever. The most productive approach is likely to be from the unit of delivery: the school, the local benefit office, the day care centre and so on. Questionnaires may form the beginning of a rapport between providers and users and this is where improvements can originate. They can help users and consumers think about what the service actually offers. Added to this, organizations should consult and respond to the needs and wishes of the staff who deliver the services: they are the people closest to the customer. This appears to be happening in some areas, as in Northamptonshire Police, although there is an acceptance that it is difficult to involve the PCs. Very often, 'front line' staff are under such pressure that they are unable to devote much time to thinking about changes. At the London office of Companies House, a junior manager collects and notes the views of staff each day and services have been changed or introduced as a direct result of these consultations.

To summarize, the following points should be considered if public sector organizations are to improve their services by making them consumer orientated:

1 Provision should ideally start from an assessment of needs and preferences gained from surveys. Often, need is only identified when consumers are asked to voice their concerns or when segments of the population are allowed a channel of communication. For example, in Community Care, local authorities will need to use market research techniques to identify need and generate supply accordingly.
2 Public and social policy should have clear objectives about what services should be achieving and why. Targets should not be just about outputs, but desirable outcomes for the service as well. The

targets for the Executive Agencies concentrate on outputs: there is little to suggest, at the moment at least, that more qualitative targets are being proposed. Market research can help policy makers clarify objectives and ensure that appropriate targets are in place that reflect users' satisfaction with the service.

3   Public sector organizations should publish information and statistics about need, provision and achievements. This is not just about marketing a service but, if the fundamental issue of choice is to be addressed, the dissemination of information is a starting point. For instance, if there is to be real choice in education, parents need to have the relevant information about each school in their area.

Clearly, market research has an important role to play in monitoring the impact of the changes in the future. Although market research has been used in various parts of the public sector over the last twenty years, its use is only beginning to be considered on a more widespread basis. Regular research should detect the benefits and disadvantages of decentralization and competition on the users and give policy makers a basis for future action and innovation. There is, of course, the danger that if the research reveals that reform has been detrimental to both the consumer and service delivery, it may be ignored if the reforms are pursued on ideological, rather than pragmatic grounds.

6　Good customer service

Service to the so-called customer

There has been a story circulating in the Cabinet Office since 1988, when Civil Servants there were trying to argue the case for improved service for the customers of public sector organizations. After much drafting and redrafting, a rather truncated document emerged, entitled 'Service to the Public' (Cabinet Office Occasional Paper, 1988, HMSO). This document contains a list of the factors which organizations need to adjust in order to provide good service, supplemented by examples of good practice from a variety of Government Departments. Rumour has it that when the correspondence first started passing among Departments, it was headed 'Service to the Customer'. Eventually, Treasury officials tired of this and a memo emerged, headed 'Service to the so-called Customer'. Whether this is an apocryphal story or not, it was recounted to typify the Treasury attitude towards customer service, far overshadowed, in their view, by a continuing need to obtain value for money. The open and hidden agenda for importing quasi-market initiatives into the public sector were alive and well and fighting in Whitehall.

For the purposes of this chapter, however, let us assume that the main thrust of these initiatives was to improve service to the users. It seems sensible to start from the assumption that, if an organization is set up to deliver a service, whether it is publicly or privately owned, it will only be successful if it delivers that service well.

It is important, therefore, to understand the principles of good service delivery and to understand that to run a successful service operation requires different managerial talents and attitudes from the needs of an administrative or allocative bureaucracy. We do not differentiate here between customer service with or without competition. Our premise is that it is possible to improve customer service whatever the environment. Without competition, the energy simply needs to come from somewhere other than the knowledge that if you provide poor service, you will go out of business as competitors step in to overtake you.

Service design

In order to deliver a good service, it is important to ask some basic questions: who, what, where, when, how and why are more than sophisticated enough for our purpose. Who is the service for (there will usually be more than one grouping of target recipients), what do they receive, when do they need to receive it, where do they need to go to get it, how is it delivered to them and why — why is it delivered in this particular what-where-when-how combination?

'What business should we be in?' is a common question asked in strategic planning. New initiatives and changes in status do provide opportunities to ask some questions about the service mix, should managers wish to take this opportunity to get back to basics. However, this chapter is about design of the service delivery system, rather than about strategic planning. The second half of this chapter goes on to look at the necessary skills, such as leadership and teambuilding, both in theory and in the practice we have discovered in public sector organizations.

Who?

It is important to try to put customers into groups. There is a market for personalized services, but individually tailored, one-off services are very expensive to supply. Mostly we look at different customer groupings when designing service operations.

This is where the first dilemma for managers in the public sector becomes apparent. There is often a split between the people who pay for a service, those who are most influential in deciding its main parameters and those who actually use it. The education of children provides an example here. The people who pay for the service are taxpayers, through central and local taxes, of whom only some will be parents. Parents, who sit on school Governing Bodies and raise funds through Parent Teacher Associations, may have some influence over the way the service is delivered, although the main parameters tend to be laid down by the providers themselves, the professional teachers. The people who actually receive the service are a different group again, the children, whose needs and desires may well be different from those expressed by the group most vocal on their behalf, the parents. In the private sector generally (although not always), the person who pays for a service and the person who receives it are often the same individual, so that the customer relationship is easier to identify and thus the delivery system easier to design.

Therefore a fundamental design issue in the public sector becomes, who do we consider to be our primary customers? To continue with the example of education, will designing a service which appeals to children (which arguably might include long play periods, short days and no homework) satisfy the other two stakeholders involved, the parents and the professionals? Probably not! The grouping of users or customers may therefore often be followed by two other steps: ranking them in importance and deciding the basic nature of the relationship. If I have different groups of interested parties who all demand something from the service I offer, but demand something different, the challenge becomes to design a service which broadly satisfies them all. One has to accept from the outset that the debate will be never-ending, because we are in fact witnessing a power struggle among contending parties, all of whom believe that they have the best ideas for the service. However, managers who make any attempt to discover what the tensions are and who seek to address them stand a better chance of survival than those who sideline or ignore the debate and wish to be guided only by their own professionalism.

In March 1991, in response to an approach from managers at London Zoo, the Government reiterated that the final tranche of £10 million which it had donated in 1988 had indeed been exactly that, i.e. final. Leaked internal memos indicating that there would be ultimately no option other than to destroy the animals immediately hit the media, with public figures lining up in the debate, either for the Zoo closing or for continuing to support it. This appears to be a classic case of failure to change an organization as the demands of its major stakeholders change. The stakeholder who subsidized (the Government) had been insisting for years that the Zoo become financially independent. In 1988 options such as moving the Zoo out of London or changing it to a theme park had been discussed. Three years later, nothing had happened. In the meantime, another important stake-holder, the visiting, paying public, had become increasingly disenchanted with the idea of caged (and possibly therefore distressed) animals, which they could see anyway on the television. In addition, the Zoo continued to be uni-dimensional, unlike its competitors such as Chessington Zoo, where varied entertainments were offered. The public voted with their feet by staying away in increasing numbers.

The middle of a crisis is not a good time to try to rally stakeholders: they need to be cultivated and well-served over the years. For example, one prominent public figure used by the Zoo to help promote its appeal for public funds was Dr David Bellamy. While he was pictured wearing a 'Save Our Zoo' T-shirt, he commented, 'We are aware of the excellent work of the Zoological Society, but it's being run like a gentlemen's club. I cannot understand how anyone can own a zoo in London and run it at a loss. It seems very strange to me when the animals are already financially sponsored by people.' (*Evening Standard*, 16 April 1991)

Let us consider the second step, defining the basic nature of the relationship with users. This in fact provides a second major dilemma for public sector managers. It may be a misnomer to call some users customers. For example, who are the customers of the prison service? Are they in fact the inmates themselves, which implies perhaps that the prison service should provide care and rehabilitation for offenders as well as custody? Or are the customers the public at large, who are being served by being protected from these same offenders? There is no simple answer, as the managers who have spent years grappling with these issues will understand. Also, because fashions change, the politically acceptable answers may also change over time. Nonetheless, managers need to confront and contain these dilemmas, because they have implications for both the design of the service and the level of service which is provided. Continuing with the prisons example above, if I decide that the public are my customers, it will be confusing for my staff to call the inmates, customers, even though it is tempting to use the rhetoric to fit with fashionable managerial thinking. However, if I do regard the inmates as my customers, this may imply a different level of service, it may imply a different design for the service delivery system and it may imply a different set of competitors: for example, am I competing with the probation service for the rehabilitation market?

It is not necessarily the fact that purchasers have a choice that makes them customers: there are plenty of private sector monopolies which I, as a customer, have to use. However, the term *customer* has rhetorical implications which outweigh a cold analysis of how many purchasers and providers there actually are in the market. Using the term implies that I expect service on my terms. It implies that I expect my views to be sought about design of the service and that these views will be reflected in the nature of the service provided. So the decision about which body constitutes an organization's customers, or primary customers, is an important one, because that group is thus allocated more power and influence over the service design. Other groupings will be fighting continually for this primary position.

A third dilemma is that some customers are not very vocal. Managers may then take on the role of champion or spokesperson for these groups or may need to recruit people to take on these roles. It is sometimes difficult for the users, who grow dependent, to voice their own views clearly. The dilemma then changes its nature, because managers need to recognize that they are on a delicate tightrope between advisor and professional. One manager told us, 'We have this sort of "mummy knows best" attitude which militates against customer service.' Another manager who had spent some time trying to resolve this conflict said to us, 'My job is to empower the stakeholder to become a more effective customer.'

So it is already apparent that what might be a fairly straightforward market segmentation exercise in the private sector is fraught with issues of principle in the public sector.

One very real advantage of importing 'market sentiment' into the public sector is that it gives managers a charter to air these issues, to open them up for public debate. So often in the past, the public sector has been regarded as some magic elixir, one spoonful enabling several conflicting targets to be met simultaneously. Now managers are expected to compile Mission Statements or Visions or Future Direction or Values Statements for their organizations. They are also expected to meet clearly defined performance targets (although the reporting procedure is still too often shrouded in mystery, so that the public is unlikely to be any the wiser about how much better or worse it is being served). This is an ideal atmosphere, or for some at the very least a window of opportunity, for clarifying some of the 'fudge' which has enshrouded the delivery of public sector services.

The basis of the Executive Agency initiative in central Government, for example, was that a contract (called a Framework Document) was to be struck between the Minister and the Agency: so many resources promised for so much output, against specified performance targets. Contracts are not supposed to be varied for their duration, which is usually three years and increased demands are to be matched by increased resources. The Project Manager (or Agency champion) Mr Peter Kemp, often refers to the initiative as 'alibi busting': managers have been saying that they can only provide good services with the resources and the tools. The Framework Documents are supposed to give managers both, so that they will no longer be able to claim an alibi from lack of either. The alternative perspective is that this is the opportunity for 'fudge busting' by the managers: an opportunity to demonstrate clearly that performance to target can be achieved, given adequate resources and managerial freedoms, which was not possible in an atmosphere of unclear and conflicting targets with inadequate resources. It therefore looks like a game where everyone wins. We come back to this issue later in the chapter, when considering managerial competencies.

There are at least three classes of individuals for whom the service is designed: customers, users and payers. These groups will not always' be distinct. The task of the management team is to distinguish between them and decide on the nature of the relationship: caring, custodial, rationing and so on, and to design the service and the service delivery system accordingly. For the purposes of the rest of this discussion, we shall use the term 'customer' to apply to all three groups, even though this may not always be true in individual cases.

What?

'What?' is an extremely interesting and complex question when designing a service. What indeed is a service? One cannot see it, touch it or smell it. It is ephemeral and intangible and often we can only tell if we like it in retrospect. You can describe my new hairdo to me, but I can only really tell if I like it or not once it is delivered: and of course, if I dislike it, it is often too late to remedy. The magenta colour that you thought would be a gentle chestnut wash has to be lived with as a constant reminder of just how bad their service was.

And if I *don't* like it, I'm going to tell ten times more people than if I *do* like it.

So in service design, we are dealing with that most difficult human attribute, perception. How do I, the customer, perceive the service? And as I cannot actually see the service, from where is this perception derived?

Managers, particularly professionals, spend a lot of time thinking about the service they provide and worrying about how to improve it. The only problem is that this consideration is often one-sided, i.e. it is the provider's perspective. It is necessary to ask the customer too. Although, as the manager, you know the service intimately, it is dangerous to assume that this knowledge means that you also know where improvements can or should be made. Time and again, carrying out customer surveys for organizations, we have found blind spots; areas where managers had not realized the impact some simple action would have on the perception their customers have of their service.

A manager who ran a local office for the Department of Social Security was trying to show customers that the service had improved. Callers were now always seen within two minutes, but when asked to complete an exit-questionnaire, customers were ticking the 'Seen within 5–10 minutes' box. This was infuriating the manager and his staff, who had devoted a lot of energy to reducing the waiting time, but it was obviously not yet appreciated. Maybe it was just a question of time-lag: it takes some time for customers to notice that things have improved. Half-jokingly, we had a brainstorming session on ways to make customers aware of the improved service. A giant clock ticking loudly behind the reception desk; a clerk trained to say brightly, 'I see that you have been waiting for one minute and 58 seconds, how may I help you?' and so on. It was quite good fun.

Then another realization slowly dawned. Perhaps customers didn't *want* to be seen within two minutes. Perhaps some of them wanted to shelter from the rain: no, this was only a minority. Well, perhaps then, other service attributes were more important to them in their decision about whether or not this was a good service. It proved to be so. A customer survey carried out by the Department in 1990, in preparation for becoming an Executive Agency in 1991, showed that what the customers wanted above all else was privacy in their discussions with the counter clerk. A creche for the children, decently decorated reception areas and even waiting time were further down the list. This was a surprise to many inside the organization.

Resources are always limited. It is important to put them where they will have most impact on customers' perceptions of the service.

How can we find out what the customer thinks? There are a number of different ways, some easier and cheaper than others. Often the first step is the hardest: actually deciding that customers have views which should be sought. Following this decision, it is often decided to use consultants to do the research and this can certainly save time if you are hard pressed. However, don't be afraid to undertake the surveys yourself: the following are some different methods.

Questionnaire

There are basically two sorts of questionnaire: those where the respondent is asked to tick boxes in order to assign values to predetermined categories; and those where the respondent is asked to respond in free form to open questions, such as 'If you were running this organization, what is the first change you would make?' Both have advantages and disadvantages.

The biggest advantage of a 'tick-box' type questionnaire is that it is easy to draw some fairly tight conclusions about the service you offer, for example '80% of our customers like the redesigned claim form OX372b'. The disadvantage is that your customers can only offer you a judgement on the service attributes about which you have asked them; you may be missing some interesting data.

The advantage of the open question style questionnaire is that you can gain insights that more structured questioning might not have produced: however, it is very difficult to process and to group the data. If I ask 100 people what they think about something, I am likely to receive 100 different answers!

Another disadvantage is that there are no trade-offs. If I am asked what I would like to change about a service, I will probably offer the view that I would like it to be cheaper, faster and more accessible. However, whether one works in the private or public sector, there is no such thing as a blank cheque. It is better to offer choices, like the matrix in Figure 6.1, so that you can see in which general direction changes need to be made. You can safely fill in the first two categories (1 is good and 9 is bad) and let them do the rest.

The best idea is probably a mixture of the two sorts of questions, so that you can test your performance against standard criteria, but also keep an open view on changes by allowing some 'Other comments' type questions. Often putting the respondent into some sort of putative position of responsibility within the organization ('If you were the Chief Executive, what would you do next') provokes more interesting responses. The

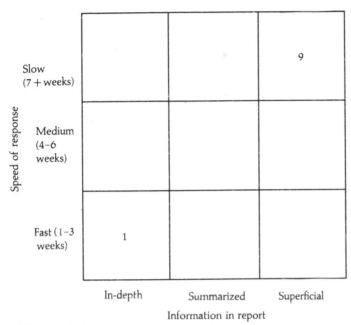

Figure 6.1

Vehicle Inspectorate Executive Agency commissioned market research which compromised between these two methods slightly differently from the way we have suggested. Their consultants undertook some pilot interviews, from which they produced a standard questionnaire. A much larger sample was then interviewed following this standard format, allowing quantitative data to be collected with a qualitative feel. Companies House commissioned research on a similar basis. HMSO also opted for qualitative interviews for the market research they commissioned.

The aim is to improve the service and this is achieved by improving the customer's perception of the service. Improvements in the managers' eyes may have little or no effect upon the customer. As a manager, you have limited resources at your disposal, including your own time and energy. It is important therefore for you to direct them where they will have the most impact on customer perception. The only way to find this out, is to ask.

Focus groups

You may not wish to survey tens of customers; or you may be puzzled by some of your findings and want to understand more. An effective way of doing this is to invite a few, say six, customers in for a discussion with you and some of your managers. One has to be careful in assessing the ideas and information gained, because the customer group you have chosen may not be representative, so it is a good idea to change the membership regularly. Of course, the influence process works in both directions in this group: not only are your managers being made more aware of what a good service looks like in your customers' eyes, but you are also able to educate your customers to use the service better. The National Weights and Measures Laboratory and Warren Spring Laboratory Executive Agencies both used focus groups as a way of better understanding their customers' needs.

MBWA

Managing by walking about (MBWA) was a popular acronym in the 1980s managerial literature. It encapsulated ideas of delegation, of letting staff get on with routine work while managers saved themselves for thinking about strategy and direction and also ideas of caring for staff: by wandering about, the manager was there as supporter and coach to empower staff to fulfil their roles to the best of their ability.

MBWA is also a very good way of gathering information. If you are doing some wandering 'front of house' as they say in the theatre, you will often hear interesting and informative comments on your service delivery system. At the same time, you are offering visible support and encouragement for your staff.

Being a customer yourself

Have you ever rung into the office to see how long it takes for the telephone to be answered? Have you ever tried to fill in one of your own forms? Have you wandered into your reception area and waited? How long did you wait? Was it a pleasant place to wait?

Asking the frontline staff

If your service business is one where some staff are actually in contact with the customer, they are often an excellent substitute for the customer in explaining what is needed. After all, they hear the complaints every day! And they want to provide a good service, both as a matter of pride and as a matter of pragmatism: fewer complaints make for happier staff as well as happier customers.

Asking frontline staff is also a bit like asking the customer: you may get some surprises.

Some Department of Social Security managers were discussing the idea of front desk staff wearing uniforms. The group was about evenly divided: half thought uniforms were a good idea, the other half declared that their staff would never wear them, mostly for safety reasons (some DSS staff have been attacked outside the office by unhappy claimants). I wondered how they were so sure of their staff's needs, so I asked them if they themselves would consider wearing a uniform. The group was about evenly divided: half thought uniforms were a good idea, the other half declared that they would never wear them.

When?

We have already seen that it is difficult to decide if you like a service before you have received it, because you cannot pick it up and inspect it. Another important feature of service operations is that very often some personal interaction is involved. This means that my customers may need to talk to my counter clerk or my receptionist or my expert, or to all three. And generally customers will want to receive service immediately, because we live in an increasingly 'immediate' world. Twenty years ago I might have written to the bank and asked them for a statement and waited for a month for a reply. Today I will post a small piece of plastic into a tiny aperture in a wall and if I do not receive a piece of paper detailing my five most recent transactions from that account and a balance statement within 10 seconds, I will be irate.

How can I solve this dilemma as a manager? A 'throw resources at it' answer leads me into the realm of individually tailored, expensive services. I can have an equal number of personnel to the number of customers expected every day, so that service is always ready and as immediate as the customer would like. Obviously, this is not the answer: it is too costly and also quite boring for the operatives, as they will spend most of the day doing nothing, waiting for their customer.

I can't store my service, so what I have to try and do is to store my customers. There are obvious ways of storing customers that we have all faced, such as queueing and appointment systems, although not all services can operate queues. The creative part of storing customers is that it needs to be done in a way which does not detract from the perception of the service as a good one. Appointments are a good idea, because they minimize the waiting time on the day; however, sometimes we have to wait a long time for an appointment to become available. Queueing can be unsatisfactory not just because of the time spent but also because of the uncertainty it creates, which is why giving people numbered tickets is a good idea, so that they have some feeling for how long they might have to wait. Managing customers' expectations is also an important part of managing the service. The Passport Office is not renowned for good service delivery. However, if one decides to go to their London office to hand in one's passport application, one knows that one may have to wait for up to four hours. The only reason the customers know that, is because the Passport Office tells them; on the passport application form and on notices in the London office. The customer therefore at least understands in advance their side of the contract being struck. However, it is not always possible to store customers in some parts of the public sector. Education must be provided from a specified age and passengers would object strongly to being stored at bus-stops, although it could be argued that the timetable itself is a surrogate appointment system. Sometimes, the best which can be achieved against a background of limited resources is awareness on the part of the customer of what the 'contract' generally entails. This is far from ideal in the many cases where public sector customers have no choice.

However, even with limited resources, a creative approach can help. The Department of Social Security, for example, decided to upgrade the person on reception in their caller offices. This speeded the service customers received, because the person seeing them was more experienced and therefore able to resolve their query, or refer them on, more quickly. This was a clever idea for another reason also. The impression we form of a service comes before we are served. Are the premises easy to find, are they pleasantly decorated, is it easy to understand what one has to do to be served? Running a service operation where there is direct customer contact can be as much about educating the customer as it is about training the staff. If I cannot find the office, if it is up a flight of stairs and there is no lift and I am in a wheelchair, if I walk in and queue at the wrong desk for half an hour only to find I am in the wrong queue . . ., then I will decide that the service is awful, even *before* I am served. I will also be quite bad tempered and may vent this on the first member of staff I see. The staff will be tired of receiving complaints from customers and will develop a shell to protect themselves. This shell may look like an uncaring attitude to the customer, who will become angrier and complain even more. This vicious circle is hard to break. The virtuous circle is one that the Department of Social Security is working hard to create: good signposting, together with pleasant premises, together with a knowledgeable first point of contact are excellent elements to help to create the impression of a good service.

It is now open to some, but not all, public services, to use price as a mechanism for manipulating the 'when'. Companies House Executive Agency, for example, has as a baseline for good service that all customers calling at their offices should have their search completed within the hour for a standard fee. However, if customers want to pay more, they can become account holders and receive the service faster via fax. Some public sector managers are demand-led and do not charge for their services: others give money to customers. Neither of these groups can use price as a mechanism for storing their customers. However, there are other routes open to them. They can try to keep more customers at arms' length, i.e. deal with them by telephone or by post. They can train the customers to supply more of the service themselves, to make it speedier, e.g. filling in their own forms. They can use third parties to provide some of the service, rather as Citizens Advice Bureaux are asked for information by potential Department of Social Security claimants. They can encourage callers with different needs to come in at different times, so that service can be speeded up by the service providers only having to deal with one sort of query at a time. They can explain to customers when the periods of peak demand are, so that those who have a choice and do not wish to wait, can use the service outside peak times. Again, the Passport Office is a good example: they explain to customers that the waiting time for a passport is much lower out of the holiday season (September to January) than from February to August.

These changes are all on the demand side, i.e. they attempt to adjust the time at which the demand arises so that service can be provided without the waiting time becoming so long that the service is perceived as poor. The other changes managers can make are on the supply side, i.e. improving the ability to supply the service when it is demanded. Employing part-time staff for peak periods, multi-skilling so that employees can switch between jobs as demand flows change, opening for longer or at times when demand is highest and using technology to speed service delivery are all examples. One of the key changes accompanying Executive Agency status is an expectation of more freedom in local recruitment of more junior staff. Companies House has also increased its opening hours so that it is open when the customers require the service, rather than at administratively convenient times.

Services cannot be, like manufactures, made for stock. It takes some juggling, some creativity and above all awareness of demand flows and ebbs to try to match supply to changed demand. If 'when' becomes a matter of queueing in frustration, the perception your customers have of your service will be poor.

The Services Manager had a problem. She kept receiving complaints about the lift service being far too slow. The capital expenditure necessary for a better lift was out of the question. Then somebody happened to remark that 'even in a doctor's surgery, there is something to do while you wait'. She had an idea. She installed a mirror by the lift. The number of complaints fell markedly. People could be seen waiting for the lift, looking in the mirror and checking their hair or their ties. Now that they had something to do, the wait didn't seem so long. 'This lift service has improved' she heard someone say.

Where?

I can send away for a wig, but not a haircut. This implies that services, or at least personal services, need to be local. This gives managers several problems. One may be managing staff at a distance, as in the case of the Vehicle Inspectorate Executive Agency, another may be performance measurement across different locations in different environments, another may be assuring service levels when no two interactions are likely to be the same, because different individuals are involved, both on the customer and on the provider side. Companies House Executive Agency for example decided to use the regional network of offices owned by the Department of Trade and Industry, in order to bring their search service closer to the customer.

Access to the service is important. Although technology can partially solve this problem, there are still many public services where the users need to be at the point of service delivery, such as schools, doctors and bus-stops. If public services are competing, a school many miles from the nearest bus route is unlikely to attract many pupils, no matter how well resourced it is and no matter how excellent its examination pass rate might be.

However, increasing use of new technology means that a service can be provided from a distance but still appear to be local. The Department of Social Security has a clerical factory in Newcastle for processing claims. Arguably, if the telephone query service there were better resourced (i.e. a more sophisticated system) then fewer people would need to call into their local offices with questions. Similarly, the fewer mistakes made with claims processed through Newcastle, the fewer callers there are at local offices. Increased use of technology has already made a difference to the level of service which they are able to offer. Now that they can pull up details of claims on a microcomputer, the telephones are no longer continually engaged as staff put the telephone down on the desk while they go and search for the relevant file. Companies House Executive Agency also supplies, as mentioned above, a fax and a telephone service for account holders. Again this offers the appearance of a local service, but delivered from a distance.

How?

How? is another interesting question when designing a service delivery system. Let us assume that the service you supply allows you to mix personal interaction with long-distance processing, rather like the Department of Social Security. As a customer, therefore, I am taught that I may receive a regular cheque for child benefit: if a problem arises, I can ring Newcastle or I can go into a local office (who then ring Newcastle for me).

The effect of this is to divorce the claim processing from the claim query activities. Such job specialization can, as we know, improve efficiency (although taken to extremes, it can also be very demoralizing for the workers). In a service system, it can improve efficiency much more than such job specialization in manufacturing. The reason for this is that, in a service business, customers get in the way. Customers do not wander around a manufacturing plant offering advice to anyone who will listen: 'ooh, if I were you, I'd attach the sprogget direct to the whingle, just think of the difference that would make to the speed'. However, as customers we are inextricably bound up in the delivery system for a service. We are free with our advice (have you ever suggested to a bank clerk a better way of dealing with your particular type of query?), which can of course provide service managers with some good ideas for improvements.

As customers, we are also not very well trained. We try to use the wrong form, we bring in the wrong documents, we do not understand the language the service provider uses. We bumble about and get in the way. Some of the organizations we spoke to tried to resolve the 'how' problem by making their communications plainer. Kent County Council has used the Plain English Society to help them to remove jargon from their documents and publications. Similarly, the Vehicle Inspectorate has tried to make its publications clear by using non-technical language.

The 'how' decision can therefore impact heavily upon the efficiency with which a service can be delivered and better communication, or training the customer, can help. It is a good idea to try to separate the personal contact side of the business from the work of the paper factory. This is also because the personnel required for the two types of work may be different, an idea we return to later in the chapter.

One moment of truth at a time

Jan Carlzon (1990), the Chief Executive of Scandinavian Air Systems, uses the phrase, 'one moment of truth at a time'. The idea is that the time actually spent in face to face interaction with a customer may be incredibly short. During a plane journey, for example, you might exchange 20 words with the steward, on boarding, on ordering a drink, on receiving your meal and on leaving the aircraft. Your job as a manager is to make sure that each of those second-long interactions leave a lasting and positive impression on the customer.

Trying to plot the 'moments of truth' in your own service has another advantage. Not only can you try to make changes which have the maximum impact on the customer, but you also gain the opportunity to look afresh at the steps your customers and providers need to take to ensure that the service is delivered. Familiarity and long-term usage can mean that we have saved intact several unimportant or irritating steps which should have been abandoned when earlier innovations were introduced.

A new manager had taken over in the Radio Vehicle Licensing Division at the Department of Trade and Industry. The unit had a poor reputation for service delivery: customers could wait up to a year for a licence, during which some of them could even go out of business. There were many things to be done and one of them was to look at the 'case action points' which an application had to go through. One such action was to write to the local authority in the area to check for objections. Not one objection had been received in ten years. The new manager therefore asked his superiors if this stage of the application could be dropped, because this step alone often caused considerable delays. The answer was 'no'.

Unperturbed, the manager quietly dropped this step in the process and a year later, informed his superiors. This time, dropping this unnecessary and time consuming step in the service delivery system was agreed.

Don't forget the extras

Implicit in what we have discussed above is the idea that each service is made up of a core service, for example, classroom lessons in a school. However, there are also peripheral services, such as school meals, the library, school trips and so on. These services may appear peripheral in your eyes, particularly if you are involved in delivering a professional service: what could be more important to children or parents than a good education? However, some parents may decide between similar schools on the basis that one provides a better transport service or clarinet lessons. Some customers may proceed under the assumption that the core service will be adequate: excellence then turns on the provision of a wide range of auxiliary services. If peripheral services can affect the choice made, then it is important to get these right too.

The people side of things

'Have a nice day now.'

We are all familiar with the idea that good customer service is about mouthing platitudes with a smile. Some of you might even have spent quite a bit of money on training programmes to learn that it is not quite that simple.

In 1988, Lord Young was about to launch the Enterprise Initiative at the Department of Trade and Industry. As part of the launch, trainers were to appear simultaneously in all of the regional offices and tell local staff about customer service and how they should treat enquiries. An enormous amount of secrecy surrounded the launch, because it was to have maximum impact. This was already causing some tension between those 'in the know' and colleagues who were not. The due date arrived and the trainers stood up and read from prepared scripts in offices across the country (to ensure uniformity across a wide geographic spread).

The initiative was not a success. Staff who felt that they had spent years building good relations with local business people were not impressed by the 'smile brigade' from Headquarters.

Are you a people service or not?

The first issue is to decide whether or not the service you provide is people intensive. Not all services are, as the example of the split between the back office processing claims and the front offices processing customers at the Department of Social Security makes plain. If the service you provide does not involve a lot of direct customer contact, then obviously 'smile' courses are irrelevant. The issue then becomes one of providing good service by improving the design of the service delivery system. Consulting the customer is still very important, because you still need to know if it is speed or accuracy or something else that the customer really wants. A fundamental assumption underlying all this is that the manager has carried out customer surveys to discover their needs. But the real skill here is one of improving the service design, by looking carefully at the steps employees have to take, by cutting out duplication and overlap and by using job specialization to the extent that it speeds up service delivery, (but not to the extent that employees become demoralized and inefficient). This requires certain key managerial skills, while managing people who have to deal with the added stress of direct contact with customers may emphasize some of these skills more than others.

How big a change is this going to be?

Bureaucracies are very good organizational structures for completing routine work, for embodying values like fairness and equity through written and formal rules and for ensuring standard outputs. They are not so good at allowing managers and employees the scope for innovation or creativity, for experimentation or for change. Systems are designed to reinforce the work patterns chosen and actions are often predicated on the assumption of a stable or largely unchanging external environment. Bureaucracies are also often large, because they grow in response to the need to process a lot of work. Jobs tend to be specialized, so that work can be completed faster and more efficiently: there may be little contact with the person fulfilling the next step in the service delivery chain, because the work has been divided into autonomous segments. For example, Volvo in Sweden was remarkable as the first car manufacturer to allow teams to work on the completion of one car at a time, rather than splitting the work up in the more usual assembly line fashion. Output was not as fast as in more traditionally designed car manufacturing plants, but there was increased job satisfaction (from workers who had the psychological reward of seeing a complete task) and quality was also held to be higher (because the workers felt that they 'owned' the product and wanted it to be the best).

Strong external controls are exercised on our public sector bureaucracies, through political processes or through lobbyists and pressure groups. High penalties are exacted for failures and strong external control tends to lead to centralization inside the organization. Because public sector bureaucracies are traditionally held to operate in stable environments, there is time for decisions to move up and down a chain of command before a conclusion is reached. When the penalty for failure is higher than that for inaction, it is safer not to act than to act and be proven wrong. A lot of energy is devoted to making sure that all angles are considered before a decision is reached: to making sure that all the paperwork is there on file in case of later problems; that all steps laid down in the manual are undertaken; that anything potentially contentious is referred up the chain of command, thus creating and reinforcing the trend towards centralization; and that information is closely guarded by individuals, both as the primary power source enhancing their own position and because individuals are wary about how this information might be used. Bureaucracies are attractive to people who like structure and orderly progression: such people are adaptors rather than innovators.

To put it more plainly, in the army they teach 'ready, aim, fire': in industry, they teach 'ready, fire, aim': and in the public sector they teach 'ready, ready, ready'. Matters are argued to a conclusion, not an outcome.

Government policies designed to implement market solutions together with popular management thinking in the 1980s led to many public sector managers being berated on training courses for their 'attitudes'. 'We have an attitude problem here' was also a common opening statement made by senior managers to consultants, as though these attitudes appear from nowhere and have to be seen off, leaving the people intact and operating 'better'. Although it is true to say that some people are psychologically better suited to working in structured, orderly surroundings, their working skills and attitudes are then shaped and moulded by the environment in which they operate. Senior managers in the Virgin Group are a good example of this. Richard Branson, the Chief Executive, role models entrepreneurship and innovation: his closest confidantes and senior managers freely admit that they are not entrepreneurial, but that they demonstrate many entrepreneurial characteristics, (like a mindset which believes that anything is possible), because this is what Richard expects of them. (He also structures his large organization into small operating segments, where everyone has an identity, a feeling of belonging and the space to take careful risks, i.e. to experiment but to protect the downside.) Similarly, the Registrar General for England and Wales, Mr Peter Wormald, values delegation and participative management. He role models these and takes every opportunity to discuss them with managers in the Office of Population, Censuses and Surveys. He is taking the slower, participative route to change management in the knowledge that such an approach breeds ownership and tends to last longer than the faster, imposed route for change.

In a bureaucracy, means can become ends. An example of this is the Executive Agency initiative in central Government. In February 1991, a briefing note for journalists listed the numbers of Agencies, together with a list of Agencies-to-be. There were at that time 34 Agencies employing about 82 000 staff, with a further 34 employing about 203 000 on the list. This briefing also stated that ... 'the objective of seeing Next Steps applied to at least half the Civil Service by the end of 1991 ... has been set'. But what difference has this plethora of Agencies made? Why are so many being created? Had the Ibbs' target of giving managers '... radical change in the freedom to manage ... (for) ... better results ... to be achieved' been met? The briefing commented that, 'Results from the Agencies are promising'. Certainly some of them have introduced some new services, but their managers have hardly been given 'radical change in the freedom to manage'. But the initiative is rolling and we are into the numbers game: it is more important to create them than that they should be creative.

One reason why means can become ends is that the systems and procedures used in bureaucracies tend to be cumbersome. With much double-checking and a high penalty for being wrong, it is easy for managers and employees to become focused on fulfilling the demands of the systems properly. Even a stable environment moves eventually, but managers can become so internally focused that they fail to detect external changes and continue with outdated or outmoded procedures. Sometimes they do detect changes, but often these new ways of operating are added to the existing ones, rather than scrapping the old when moving to the new.

This is why the role of customers is so important. It is to them that the organization is set up to deliver services. Bringing that external environment alive by empowering their voice in planning the service design can keep employees focused on the ends — why they are doing what they do and which might be the best way to achieve this — rather than on the means, having been carefully through every prescribed step in the procedure.

Much management literature in the 1980s suggested that getting close to the customer was one way of ensuring survival, of keeping adaptation alive in a changing market place. This advice was directed towards private sector companies, whose managers appear just as capable of focusing on the means as the managers of public sector bureaucracies, despite market forces and the presence of competitors. Writers like the now world-famous Tom Peters recommended other ideas as well, like taking risks, acting first and seeing if ideas work through experimentation. These ideas tended to be pumped wholesale at private and public sector managers alike. For example, the Department of Social Security Executive Agency espoused four core values when it was launched in April 1991: Caring for Customers; Caring for Staff; A Bias For Action; and Value For Money. Aucoin (1990) writes that a '"bias for action" derives from a perception that centralized organizations suffer from self-inflicted constipation brought about by paralysis-by-analysis or the getting-ready-to-get-ready syndrome'. A bias for action *is* much harder to achieve in a bureaucracy where rules and procedures must be gone through first and also much harder to achieve in the public sector, with its high penalty for failure.

One could also ask a supplementary question: do we, as customers, actually *want* our public sector providers to demonstrate a bias for action? It probably depends on how the term is defined and enacted. I do not want a counter clerk at the Department of Social Security to be innovative when I present a claim; I just want what I am entitled to, the same as a similar customer. However, I *do* want them to think carefully about, and react to, my needs.

Ensuring good customer service from the back office

What steps do managers need to take to improve customer service where the customer is never seen, in the back office or processing section?

Meet the customer

If, as we argue here, customer focus is important, it is doubly important in the back office. When there is no necessity to meet the customer, it is even easier to concentrate on completing the procedures correctly rather than thinking about their impact on the end receiver. Try to make sure that the staff in the back office meet the customer, either socially, through job rotation with staff who do meet the customer, as part of the market research effort (e.g. focus groups) or through some other means. Your staff will then become the spokesperson for the customer within the organization and also have a clear focus about why they carry out the operations they do. Our research into Executive Agencies shows that still, too often, clerical staff have little idea about the overall purpose of the Agency for which they work and even less idea about some of the changes being made and their purpose. Yet very often it is just these people who are the primary producers of the organization. It is vital to harness their energy and interest.

Meeting the customer helps the service designer, but also helps the customer by opening up a channel of communication for them. For instance, some of the subsidiary bus companies took the unilateral decision of placing the names of the garage general managers on the buses in order to encourage comments about the service. Many managers talk of having an open-door policy or headteachers making themselves available to parents on open days and so on. Experience at British Airways shows us that the most disgruntled customers are those who are badly served and have no direct outlet for complaining to those responsible. It seems that we can treat customers quite badly as long as we demonstrate our concern subsequently to put matters right!

Think again about what you do

We said at the start of this chapter that we were not suggesting that managers should ask fundamental questions about *what* they do, but rather only about *how* they do it. Sometimes it is difficult to differentiate between the two, because in thinking through the steps involved in service delivery, it can become apparent that some peripheral services you provide are no longer required by your customers. As always, knowledge about your customers and what they like and dislike is a prerequisite for this strategy.

Many organizations, in both the public and private sectors, are using Total Quality Management as a way of eliminating overlap and duplication in their service delivery procedures. The ideas underlying Total Quality Management are powerful and potentially extremely helpful.

Total Quality Management tells managers to involve the people who actually carry out the work in thinking afresh about what they do, and why, and in redesigning the procedures where necessary. It tells managers to let people find creative ways of working across functional or job boundaries, because working in tiny, independent cells and referring decisions up and down a chain of command takes too long in today's faster moving world. It tells managers to encourage people to take responsibility for what they do themselves, rather than assuming it is somehow the manager's responsibility. All these messages imply a fundamentally different way of thinking and acting in a public sector bureaucracy.

Because this implies that more decisions need to be taken laterally across the organization, fewer levels of hierarchy will be needed. Her Majesty's Stationery Office Executive Agency implemented in April 1991 a restructuring exercise which reduces the effective layers of management in their organization to four. It implies that more authority will be delegated (to accompany the responsibility that often seems to drift down the hierarchy more easily) so that staff cannot only propose, but also implement their ideas. A staff suggestion scheme with the 'winners' being chosen periodically by some manager up the hierarchy misses the point entirely. To create ownership, the staff involved must be able to propose and act as well. It implies that the psychological reward systems inside the organization need to change radically, to reward experimentation rather than stasis. Companies House Executive Agency seems to have achieved this. One of the comments made to us was: '... before, you couldn't do it unless it was in the rulebook; now it is, you can try it because it *isn't* in the rulebook'. This is a phenomenal advance in thinking, achieved for some of the reasons we set out in Chapter 3 and return to in Chapter 7.

As with the staff suggestion scheme, some organizations miss the point and believe that Total Quality Management is about conformity to BS 5750. While this might be helpful, if this is *all* it is, it will simply have replaced one set of externally imposed rules and regulations with another. Total Quality Management, or TQM as it is more popularly known, is simply a useful acronym for good management. Let the people see the purpose in what they do, let them understand what it is for and how it contributes to the whole and let them take responsibility for what they do. Give them the matching authority to take decisions and implement ideas to improve their own performance and thus the overall performance of the organization. Clever managers are using TQM as a way of forging new psychological contracts with their workforce.

A lot has been written about the psychological contracts that workers form with their employers: they act because they are frightened to do otherwise, because they respect the people they work for, because there is something in it for them or because they associate so closely with the aims and values of the organization that they are self-motivated, because they themselves hold the same fundamental beliefs and values. People who work in the voluntary sector are often held to have the latter, 'ideal' psychological contract with their employing organization: their employment is simply a way of expressing and enacting their beliefs. They have internalized the organization's value system.

Smart managers in the 1990s are trying to extend the scope and spread of the internalized psychological contract. If it can be achieved, it replaces manuals and written rules with unspoken values which drive how decisions are taken. As the Deputy Chief Executive of Her Majesty's Stationery Office Executive Agency succinctly puts it: 'It's a hearts and minds job'.

Networking

The implication is that the manager focuses less on the nitty gritty of getting day-to-day work completed: these tasks are delegated. Lots of managers do try to withdraw from such activities, but then need to find an alternative, but equally useful, role. One Chief Executive told us: 'It took me a year to implement the reorganization, but then the temptation was to become involved in the daily work. I resisted, because my job was to adopt a more strategic role.' Certainly, the idea of managers thinking about the future, rather than the present, and of drawing a picture of the future (or vision) for employees, is a popular recommendation. Unfortunately, even with fewer tiers in the hierarchy ('delayering' is the popular parlance), not all managers can always be involved in strategic planning. One important task for the newly liberated manager is nonetheless to undertake environmental monitoring on an individual basis by maintaining contacts outside the organization. This can mean finding out what collaborators are doing, investigating the competition, looking at similar organizations elsewhere, meeting important customers, or any combination of the above. Even public sector organizations can no longer rely upon a steadily changing environment: managers need to be alert for the changing tide so that they can catch it on the top of the wave, rather than drowning.

Leadership

There is a great deal written about leadership, but much less is understood. As Henry Mintzberg said in a research seminar at the end of 1990, we have been researching into leadership for 90 years and are still no further forward in our understanding.

A great deal has also been written by popular writers like Warren Bennis about the difference between leadership and management. Broadly, somewhat of a caricature of this strain of literature is that managers are rather boring implementers of policy, while leaders are exciting creative people who enjoy innovation. We have all experienced the reverse, i.e. boring leaders and charismatic managers.

We believe that there is in truth little difference between good managers and good leaders. Good managers and good leaders both try to motivate their staff, both try to engage them in the work they are doing, both try to encourage them to improve. An interesting piece of longitudinal research into what staff wanted from their managers, carried out over 25 years to 1986, concluded that they wanted them to be creative, caring and decisive. Broken down into behaviours, this meant that they wanted them to take a forward-looking approach, to take decisions *when* needed and to care about the progress and development of their staff. These needs had changed very little over the 25 years of the study. Being decisive and forward looking often seems to come more easily to managers. It is caring for staff which is often overlooked in the daily scrum of getting the service delivered. Managers recognize the importance of this intellectually: but good management is not a theoretical exercise. In one of the Executive Agencies we talked to, all the senior managers have been on a Strategic Leadership course. The results from our survey show it to be the most undemocratic and highly centralized organization of all those we studied. No doubt the managers found the course interesting and useful: but there is something about how they are structured and how they themselves feel controlled from outside the organization which means that they are unable yet to implement these ideas.

Caring for staff can have a variety of definitions. It is not generally about a lax approach to performance delivery combined with remembering to ask how the family is. It is a lot to do with remembering that individuals performing the job are likely to know more about it than you do, so that it is worthwhile cherishing their opinions and advice; it is about making sure that people are equipped to do their jobs, i.e. have adequate information as well as training; it is about listening and encouraging people to take their own decisions; it is about letting go of information as a power resource. Another of the Executive Agencies we surveyed showed that senior managers had mastered the art of delegating real power and autonomy down the line. However, they had done this in a rather autocratic way, communicating little with the workforce who then felt unsupported and uncared for. There had also been little training for the employees now expected to take over areas such as budgeting. The senior managers were puzzled and concerned by our findings, nor could they understand how people could not feel empowered by being given so much of the power (over decision-making) which they themselves valued. It was simply because the 'caring' part had somehow been left out of the package. It is also worth remembering, as a senior manager or leader, that one of the reasons why you rose to the top of the organization is because you are motivated by being in control and by taking decisions which affect others. Not all people are motivated by this: some, particularly those without work ambitions, are keen to do a good job, but not to run the organization. Giving them increased responsibility without clear parameters and lots of support can therefore appear threatening rather than empowering.

Role modelling

An idea closely linked to that of leadership, is role modelling. It appears that one of the easiest ways for people inside organizations to learn new ways of working is if they see others, people in positions of power, working in the new ways. This is a clear indication that things really have changed and that there is some reality in the rhetoric. One manager we know, in the Department of Social Security, borrowed money from High Street shops to make payments to claimants, when he would otherwise have been prevented from doing so by strike action. As he said to us, then all he had to worry about was paying the shops back when Monday morning arrived. Not only did he keep his job, he was also elevated to membership of a select group of managers which met monthly at Headquarters in London, considering what Executive Agency status might mean for their work. This new way of working, of risk taking, was therefore rewarded. This also points up another lesson.

Often, when we speak of rewards in the context of discussing organizations, there is a temptation to think immediately of financial rewards. Even in private sector organizations, the ability to reward financially is restricted to a few managers. However, the ability to reward psychologically, by praise, by offering membership, is open to a far wider range of managers. This sort of reward is too often a sadly under-utilized resource in organizations.

Role modelling is not something which seems to occur to public sector managers. Because people inhabit a 'post' and a 'grade', there is less personal contact with the job and therefore with the people who report to that 'post'. It is not that public sector managers are unpleasant; on the contrary, they tend to be well-educated, thinking people who are often concerned with ideas of public service. However, the 'post' exists before they get there and continues to exist after they leave: it is not personal to them, it is independent of them and may even lie vacant before they arrive or after they leave, but it still continues to exist. They therefore tend to underestimate the impact that they can have on their staff: they are just occupying a 'post' to the best of their ability and (wrongly) expect others to be similarly motivated.

Teambuilding

The foregoing implies a far greater emphasis on lateral links throughout the organization, rather than up and down a chain of command. It implies that decisions will emerge as a result of discussions involving people doing the work and perhaps also people affected by the work even if not directly involved in the delivery. In short, it implies a far greater emphasis on people working together in groups. If they are willing to devote the extra energy needed, they can also become a team.

A team implies something more than a group, because it implies a basic level of agreement, even if unspoken, about aims and beliefs. It is not only safe, but also rewarding, to debate within a team, because richer ideas are gained. In a group, argument can appear threatening. A team implies a level of trust and a high value placed on working together and cooperation: an understanding that differences among team members mean that the tasks will probably be better completed.

There are many diagnostic tools on the market designed to tell you what your preferred role in a team is likely to be and the strengths and weaknesses of this role. These are valuable as an aid to get discussion started, about individual differences, about what your team needs to become more successful, about what your team does well and how it might improve. This really is all they are. The hard work obviously comes from the team members themselves. They need to feel committed to the aims of the team, to feel an affinity with other team members, to feel confident that they can improve performance and to see that improvement happen. For this, the team will need performance measures in place, or will need to create some, so that success and progress can be charted. It means that the team members will need to spend sufficient time together to build the trust necessary for interpersonal disclosure and building excellent working relationships: not all of this time will be spent working. Some of it may be spent socializing, or talking about the nature of the work, rather than doing the work. For the manager or team leader, it implies allowing time for informal meetings, making sure that the team meets regularly and supporting individuals as they try to understand others. This is a far cry from the rational manager, who believes that her or his job is to set objectives for others and see that they are met.

Ensuring good customer service in front of house

This section started out discussing improving service delivery out of sight of the customer. Some of your people may, however, have face-to-face contact with customers. What further managerial skills does this imply?

Coming into direct contact with customers is extremely taxing work. Customers are not always polite and indeed, if your service delivery systems are not up to the job, they may well be angry by the time they reach your representative. Their needs may vary widely and they either may not be, or may not wish to be, very clear in their requirements. This implies special skills on the part of these staff. They certainly need to be extremely knowledgeable about all the services you offer and about how they inter-relate. They need to be able to remain calm despite trying circumstances. They need to be sensitive to what *isn't* said, as well as to what *is* said. They need to feel genuine empathy for the customers they face. Their ability to do this will depend crucially on the support you give them.

> When British Airways was privatized, the company carried out customer research. This showed that the impression customers had, was of a haughty, autocratic, uncaring organization. As customers they felt 'processed', rather than dealt with as human beings. And of course, flying can be a terrifying experience for some; just the time when they need to feel a human level of support.
>
> However, the most revealing part of the research was that it soon became apparent that the front-line staff, those in touch with the customers, felt exactly the same about their managers. They felt uncared for, undervalued, in a climate of 'do as I say, not as I do'. And it was just these feelings which they were transmitting on again to the people with whom they had contact, i.e. the customers.

It is a good idea to rotate those who have to deal with customers. Not only does this keep all staff alive to the end-purpose of what they are doing, but it also allows those on the 'front line' some time to recuperate emotionally. In some services in which there is no 'back office', such as education, other ways of allowing staff to recuperate are needed.

The challenge for managers

There is no denying that the challenge facing managers trying to adopt these new ways of working is immense.

Davies and Snell of Lancaster University undertook a study which reported in November 1986: it covered 100 managers spread across five departments in two local authorities, a similar number of managers in one Civil Service Department, a number of senior managers in the Health Service and included longitudinal data from a small number of informal contacts. Their paper was called *The Process of Disillusionment: A Block to Creativity in Managers*. The following are some extracts from the paper. 'Managers often seem to have lost the will and vision to deal with the complexity involved in the public sector ... a sense of absurdity and unreality when tasks given are seen as covering up political inconsistencies or as implementing devious power ploys. Boredom and a sense of wasting time on trivia stems from work which is seen as confined to routine procedures ... Harshness, suspicion and authoritarianism in hierarchical relationships distort communication between people on different grades ..."Once we were a penny out on the accounts. We were forced to get it right ... It made me determined to change things ... It was obsessive there." '

Of course, 1986 is a long time ago. Perhaps some progress has been made since, but the dead cold hand of conservatism was also apparent in some of our research.

Of the five Executive Agencies we looked at, two seemed to have made some real advances and we spell out the reasons for this in our proposed taxonomy in Chapter 3. Another two of the Agencies were less than enamoured with our findings and the Chief Executives wrote polite letters explaining that they thought it was difficult to extrapolate general rules from the few staff we had interviewed and that they would be unhappy to see our findings broadcast. We could quite understand this: we had carried out qualitative interviews with a limited number of staff and we would no doubt have felt the same in their position. Sadly, from their responses, it appeared further that they refused to accept the summary of what their own staff had to say about how they felt about the change to Agency status. Not only therefore did they refuse to acknowledge what they heard publicly, they further lost the opportunity to make some real changes by listening to what their staff were saying in private.

The old way of closing ranks to protect themselves was apparent in their written response to us. One sentence in each of the two letters read: 'I should, however, be very reluctant to see the report or its findings transmitted more widely. It contains errors, both of fact and of perception and, notwithstanding the reminder (point made) in your letter that the interviewees were reporting perceptions, this distinction would soon be lost, I fear, in any wider publication.' These sentences were identical apart from the one exception of the alternative words in brackets. The Ibbs Report recommended 'radical change in the freedom to manage'. Chief

Executives are supposed to run their own organizations without interference, safeguarded by a Framework Document which has a three-year life, are supposed to be directly answerable to Parliament and are rumoured to earn up to £100 000 a year. Yet it appears that someone still writes their letters for them, that the ranks still close obstinately against critical review. What hope is there for more junior managers to adopt noble slogans like 'A Bias for Action' if back-watching is still the name of the game? How can they demand that their managers learn new ways of working, if they refuse to acknowledge that there is no such thing as an 'error of perception', but simply that some of their staff are not as convinced as they apparently are of the advantages that Agency status is supposed to confer? These organizations have not yet learnt to benefit from open exchange or to value differences.

This was not a universal finding. Some of the staff in Executive Agencies are clearly enjoying tremendously having new authority and are exercising it to the full. In London Buses Limited, in the schools in Kent and in the Northamptonshire police, there was also general enthusiasm for the reforms. There was scope for flexibility and innovation along with the recognition that change was a learning process for all, a gradual evolution. These organizations were happy with our findings, reflecting the degree of autonomy they had achieved while remaining part of the public domain. There is scope, albeit more limited for some than for others, for managers across the board to start adopting some of the new ways of working for a different decade for a different public sector.

7 Making change happen

'What we are seeing at the moment ... is, frankly, nothing less than a revolution in management in the Civil Service ... an opportunity, I believe, to give managers and staff far more scope than ever before to achieve greater effectiveness and greater value for money; ... and above all perhaps far greater scope for what we are there for in the first place — delivering a better service to the customer ... Agencies in no sense are just another bureaucratic binge of reorganization — that is not what Agencies are about. They are meant to provide a better service ...'. (The Rt Hon John Major, Prime Minister, at the launch of the Benefit and Contribution Agencies, 10 April 1991.)

In this example, the Prime Minister is talking specifically about Executive Agencies, only one type of public sector organization considered in this book. However, Mr John Major's idea of a Citizens' Charter has been widely reported in the press and was also referred to elsewhere in this speech. The Citizens' Charter is to apply to all services across the public sector and, as the Prime Minister spelt out on this same occasion: '... means better accountability to people (from) the public services that they use in their everyday lives ...'.

We have spent a lot of time in this book introducing different public sector organizations and talking about what has happened to them over the last three years. Some managers reading this book may already have identified the organization most like their own and have started making comparisons.

Comparisons are interesting and useful. However, much more useful is to be able to use the lessons in some way, so that the practising manager can avoid some of the pitfalls that others have made, or take advantage of some of the innovations others have managed to introduce. This chapter therefore attempts to pull together some of the diverse threads in this book and to produce a map, or schema, so that readers can undertake the sort of diagnostic appraisal that a consultant might perform. This map is illustrated in Figure 7.1.

It cannot be over-stressed that for each manager, the situation or context they face must determine the overall use of the map.

For example, there was some research undertaken at London Business School in the 1980s on strategic change in the UK cutlery industry, (Grant, 1987). Four strategies were assessed, all of which could apply equally to the public sector: namely, cost reduction through capital investment;

product differentiation; up-market movement into higher quality product segments; and broadening market scope through product and geographical diversification. The results were surprising. There was, for example, a *negative* relationship between investment in plant and machinery and sales, profitability and sales growth. Interviews with managers in the companies revealed why: the firms which had invested heavily in units of modern equipment were unable to produce long enough product runs to use the new equipment efficiently. Similarly, improved quality or shifts upmarket were accompanied by significant reductions in return on capital. This surprising result occurred because too many firms tried to move up-market at the same time, so that market sector became crowded.

Perhaps this simply proves again the vulnerability of generic strategies, or why organizations need managers, for it is only managers who are in a position to monitor what else is happening in the environment and to make appropriate adjustments.

However, managers are not simply benign units of change: they can also be malign units of stasis. It is important that managers themselves are 'sold' on the idea of change, that they feel involved in, and committed to, the 'new tomorrow'. Our research has not found any managers who are trying to thwart change. We have, however, found examples of managers being underused, still being treated as cogs in a production cycle, rather than being fully utilized so that their energies can be unleashed as champions of change. In the longer term, this can lead to disaffection and engender resistance to change. We have also found managers facing externally imposed change which they are finding hard to align with the internal needs of the organization and the external needs of customers. We hope that the results from our research can help them to find the alignment which some others are further on their way to finding.

The levers for change

Politicians and senior managers giving policy advice cannot rely simply upon sending a memo to ensure change in large, bureaucratic and politically sensitive organizations. They need to use other levers. The main lever for change in the Government's eyes, since 1979, has been heavily located in market initiatives. Competition has been introduced at various levels: through privatization, through subcontracting work out to bidding organizations and through restructuring and requiring managers to reapply for their former jobs (often, however, with enhanced responsibilities) in competition with each other. None of these levers has been perfectly applied. For example, privatization has sometimes been introduced without any concomitant increase in competition; subcontracting

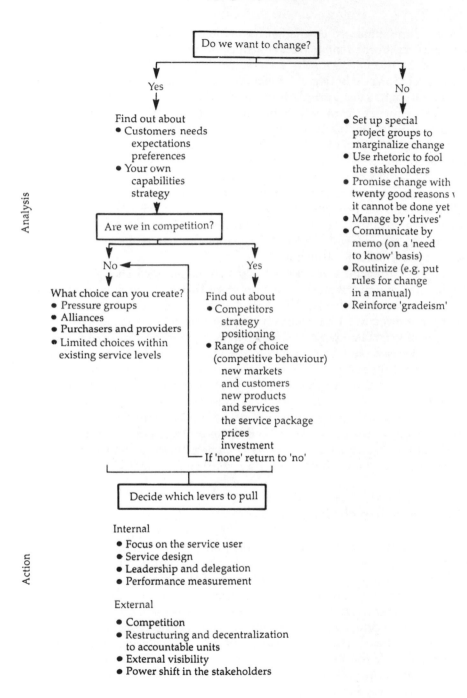

Figure 7.1   The four 'A's

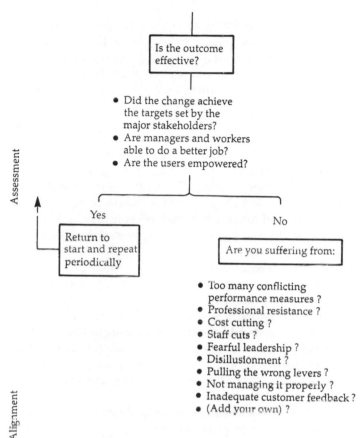

Assessment

Is the outcome effective?

- Did the change achieve the targets set by the major stakeholders?
- Are managers and workers able to do a better job?
- Are the users empowered?

Yes

Return to start and repeat periodically

No

Are you suffering from:

- Too many conflicting performance measures ?
- Professional resistance ?
- Cost cutting ?
- Staff cuts ?
- Fearful leadership ?
- Disillusionment ?
- Pulling the wrong levers ?
- Not managing it properly ?
- Inadequate customer feedback ?
- (Add your own) ?

Alignment

Dilemmas now facing you are a clue to misalignment. Have you pulled one lever and forgotten another, e.g. decentralization without performance measurement?

Figure 7.1   (*continued*)

has not always been carefully monitored, or has reduced costs at the expense of service levels. With Executive Agency status, the changes have sometimes been labelled erroneously as introducing competition, resulting in disillusionment from managers who want to operate their organizations as 'businesses' and then find that legislation, or a requirement to preserve old public sector values like equity, intervene.

There is no doubt that competition can be an important impetus to change. Managers in British Telecom have told us that it was not privatization, but competition from Plessey in equipment supply and from Mercury in services which were the real spur to increasing efficiency. A senior manager at the Civil Service College Executive Agency told us that having to 'earn' their living, when they moved to direct repayment from Government Departments, had the major impact on employees. Managers from British Waterways Board have made similar statements. However, it is not always possible, or sensible, to introduce competition. Schooling is just one example of current debate. Is it sensible to employ School Heads as expensive administrators, or to divert energy towards marketing and competitive activities which might better be devoted to increasing the standard of education? Is competition really the best, or only, way of improving standards? Economists add the further cost argument of natural monopoly. In some cases, for example with complex infrastructure needs, the most cost-effective form of organization is a monopoly: railways would be an example. Economies of scale argue for only one organization, with subsidiary controls (like Monopolies' Legislation) to ensure that the benefit of these economies is not then squandered through complacency encouraging lax service delivery or over-pricing.

The real question must be, can equivalent service improvements be achieved without introducing competition? Further, is competition alone a sufficient prerequisite for improving service levels? Our research shows that there are many levers for change, of which competition is only one, and that it is often necessary to use more than one lever to effect lasting change. Further, not only do companies which go out of business demonstrate that competition is not a universal panacea; but also our research shows that some monopolies are able to achieve significant change, by concentrating on other levers.

Internal levers for change

These are the levers within managerial control. Managers may choose to use these to try to align internal organizational reality with external imposed changes.

Some books on managing change (for example Greiner and Schein,

1988) only consider Organizational Development (OD) issues when considering change. The levers for change are therefore *internal*, or come from within the organization. The emphasis is on ideas like power, allegiances, training and leadership. The importance of some of these issues has indeed been reinforced by our research.

Focus on the service user

Some of the organizations we studied were, and remain, monopolies. Nonetheless, their managers have taken the view that, just because their customers have to use them, does not imply that they can be complacent about how their services are delivered. They, together with other non-monopolistic public service providers, have therefore taken care to consult their customers about how the service delivery currently provided matches up to their users' needs and to try to make changes where appropriate. An example here is the Civil Service College Executive Agency. They did some market research to find out what their customers liked most and least about their service. They were interested to learn from this that one of the major benefits listed by customers was being able to exchange ideas with fellow professionals from other Departments. This insight allowed the College lecturers to change course design to allow more significant periods of discussion on key topics with fellow course participants.

It is not just customers who benefit of course. The point of allowing the service deliverers to meet their customers, to see the 'end product' of their labours, is to inspire and motivate managers and staff alike. This is particularly true of the service deliverers who habitually inhabit the back office and who therefore rarely have this exposure. People generally want to do a good job: allowing them the luxury of seeing what a good job looks like, through their customers' eyes, is some of the best training available.

We do not wish to triviailize the debate we started in Chapter 6: an extremely important precursor to all of this is to decide who the customer is. For example, there is no point in improving the lives of prisoners in their cells at the expense of guarding the safety of the general public. Indeed, in some circumstances it might be better to avoid the popular rhetoric of calling service users, customers, at all. It is not for us to prescribe where those situations might arise. Even less is it for us to tell some organizations where the term 'customer' has been usefully employed in order to motivate staff, that being a customer implies some level of choice and that if their users have no choice, then they are not 'real' customers. These arcane debates rightly belong inside educational establishments, rather than outside with practitioners. It may matter little what you call your service users: however, the term used should imply respect and a desire to provide good service. Using the term customer also implies, of course, that this body is the main recipient of your attentions and receives service first and above all others. One of the major reasons underlying the Executive Agency initiative was just this: that service delivery should be divorced from strategy, because senior managers spent too long worrying about protecting and advising Ministers and too little on worrying about the service they were delivering.

This brings us to accountability. While the Prime Minister's concern to improve direct accountability to service users is commendable, this has to be balanced with accountability to the wider population of the country, as expressed through Parliament. This means that at some point, managers may feel frustrated because they can see service improvements which their customers or users would like, but which have not been ratified by Parliament. This conflict has not yet arisen, as far as we are aware, in the organizations we studied. However, managers may find themselves primarily seeking feedback from service users on the most effective way of delivering the current range of services, rather than introducing new services, because these might need Parliamentary sanction. It might, for example, highlight a social imperative not yet recognized or accepted: this information should nevertheless provide invaluable feedback for Parliament on further changes. Nor will this conflict be so apparent in those public sector organizations which trade, i.e. where what they provide is covered by income, rather than by statutory fee. An example here would be Her Majesty's Stationery Office Executive Agency, where new services have been introduced in line with customer demand. Monopolies like the Benefits Agency, which essentially give money away rather than earn it, may be more limited in the extent to which they can innovate.

It is vitally important for managers in different situations to take these limiting factors into account, rather than being swayed by the rather general rhetoric offered at political and senior levels.

Service design

Encouraging service providers to look critically at the stages in the service delivery process is often called Total Quality Management. It is a way of encouraging employees to take charge of what they do. However, to work, it requires equal commitment on the part of managers up to the highest level. People will cease to be interested if their ideas are not implemented. Better still, they should be given responsibility both for improvement and for implementation, wherever possible without the 'vetting' implied by the ubiquitous staff suggestion scheme. We predict that entirely new structural forms will emerge from successful implementation of ownership and internalization of cultural norms as the psychological contract with workers engaged in bureaucratic endeavour.

Delegation

We use this term to imply the downwards movement of authority and responsibility within the organization, rather than a restructuring decision taken outside the organization and imposed upon it. We found a higher level of motivation in managers and employees where a visible and changed degree of decentralization had been implemented. This expressed itself in terms of understanding the changes taking place, a heightened awareness of the reasons and need for change and an active part being taken in implementation through their increased responsibilities.

Leadership

The public sector has a new-found interest in leadership, previously considered the prerogative of the elected leaders of the country. However, senior civil service, NHS and local authority staff are now being encouraged to believe that effective managerial leadership from within the organization is as important in achieving goals as the more rhetorical leadership offered by political leaders. This is a natural development following initiatives to create smaller, more 'business-like' units, an increasing emphasis on personal objectives building up to meet organizational goals and more publicity being given to the doings, sayings and recruitment of senior public sector managers.

Thus, management trainers all over the country have found themselves exhorting public sector managers to empower others, to delegate and to Manage By Walking About.

The sad truth is that one cannot teach leadership but only raise awareness in potential leaders of the issues involved. The even sadder truth is that a new style of leadership *is* important in these new style organizations. The bureaucratic model of 'occupying a role or post' resulted in quietly dedicated individuals arriving and doing a job for a while and then moving on, perhaps to be replaced or perhaps, in more cost constrained times, not being replaced, with their 'post' thus left vacant.

Ownership was not encouraged nor even personal recognition. It is an enormous leap to move from that to a highly visible and personalized commitment to change an organization and to link one's own fate to one's success or failure in so doing. And it is something which leaders cannot achieve on their own.

There are two sorts of help the new-style public sector leader needs, one from above and one from below. Let us start with help from above. The high penalty for failure exacted from our public sector, coupled with a bureaucratic mode of organization, naturally resulted in public sector managers and leaders keeping a low profile, following rules and, because of frequent job moves, not becoming too committed to any one area of work. Leadership requires the opposite. Further, because of the high penalty for failure a curious counter-culture often developed, as a defence mechanism. This counter-culture does not learn from failure, but instead derides it as unimportant, as a psychological defence mechanism. For example, a senior administrator at the Civil Service College Executive Agency ran a course for even more senior managers which was a resounding failure. The individual concerned turned this into a joke, something to be told and re-told. If one laughs at something, it cannot be important and therefore one cannot be damaged by it. However, neither can one learn from it. Therefore more senior managers and politicians need to allow failure as a learning process, so that leaders of public service organizations can role model openness rather than defensiveness. This may not be possible, if we accept that societal values bound or limit organizational values and that our society also regards failure either as a joke or as a disaster.

What support does the leader need from below? There is of course no leadership without following. While leaders need to delegate real authority and to allow their followers to experiment as they themselves need to be allowed to experiment, they need support from their followers in order to do so. Followers need to recognize and accept leadership. This may sound trivial, but course leaders at the Civil Service College still debate with course participants about whether a (civil) servant can be a leader. Some Chief Executives, like Michael Bichard at the Benefits Agency and David Durham at Companies House, are public sector but not *central* public sector: not 'of the culture' and therefore somehow expected (or allowed?) by staff to have more of an impact. Followers also need to use their expertise to support leaders in their attempts to adopt a leadership role of direction setting and encouragement, so that leaders are not tempted to second-guess their followers and try to become involved in daily routines. In some cases, this may mean questioning the leader's views and certainly questioning their right to re-work decisions already taken at a lower level.

Performance measurement

Performance measures on both sides of the economy are often vague and concentrated on inputs rather than on outputs or outcomes. People may spend a lot of time and energy defending their lack of performance measurement because what they do is 'unmeasurable': policy advice is an example often quoted. This may be because they are debating the principle, rather than the actuality. Managers who do not expend energy on trying to measure, both qualitatively as well as quantitatively, what they do, are missing an enormous opportunity for more effective service delivery.

> The new manager had inherited an operation where service delivery was variable (between two months and a year from case to case). Backlogs were an accepted part of life and newcomers soon learnt, through informal induction procedures, that it was a waste of time trying to eliminate them (after all, old hands had already tried this once). So the new manager suggested that they try to measure what they did and agree an acceptable output level. There was some resistance, but the manager persisted: in particular, by delegating the task of measurement to those who performed the work, on the not unnatural assumption that those who do the work are best placed to measure it. Eventually, and painfully, an acceptable measurement scheme was devised. Output doubled immediately '... and that was before I brought in the computers ...', the manager explained. Teams started to compete with each other: a notice on one door read 'The A Team: the Backlog Busters'. On the day the computers first arrived, one clerk completed a week's target in one day, 'Just to show that I could do it'.

Performance measurement has demonstrated its power again during our research. The focus on outputs has been instrumental in pulling people together in a common cause and in motivating them by allowing them to see that they are doing a good job.

External levers for change

Other writers, e.g. Pettigrew (1987) look at what is happening in the environment to promote change inside organizations. Our research uncovered some ideas in this area too, which were tentatively explored in Chapter One. Because these levers are *external* they are, by definition, imposed on the organization rather than being directly within managers' control. Managers may seek to invoke, to align with, or to defend against these changes.

Increasing competition

A competitive threat somehow has more meaning than a general exhortation to 'maximize profitability' or to 'provide value for money'. It is not simply that managers lack the rationality to achieve these goals, but also that these goals are often vague, are not supported by sub-goals inside the organization or are ill-supported by contradictory sub-goals. It is easier to concentrate on the competition, 'the enemy'. This has certainly been the proclaimed method of choice of the Conservative Government since 1979.

Where real competition exists, it is certainly a spur to improvement. Companies House and Her Majesty's Stationery Office Executive Agencies are two examples of where increased competition has had an impact once it has been communicated inside the organization. Obviously people have to realize that they face competitors, which implies monitoring the environment outside the organization and communicating inside the organization. One reason why many public sector managers currently feel so beleaguered or so convinced that they are facing exponential change of a type never encountered before, is that they are not used to monitoring the environment, nor being 'externally' aware. Previously, the environment has felt more secure or less changeable. Sometimes the competition *is* apparent, in highly competitive markets. The competition faced by public sector bodies is often more limited (because if private sector suppliers exist, the public sector body is required to exit from that market) and less aggressive, because often competitors are other public sector bodies and ideas of collaboration, rather than competition, are hard to suppress. For example, the Chief Executive of the Civil Service College Executive Agency met some competitors from the former Training Agency and shared her vision and strategy with them freely: perhaps more freely than the organization's new competitive position might deem wise. It therefore again becomes a key task of managers and leaders to make the competitive threat clear. Companies House Executive Agency has achieved this with some impact, by commissioning market research specifically comparing their performance, in their customers' eyes, to that of 'competitors', and sharing this information widely inside the organization.

However, the proviso about real competition is an important one. Acting as though there were competitors when none exist in reality can backfire. While staff may not realize the extent of competition, or understand in detail their competitors' strategies, they are usually aware of whether competition exists or not! It is better to use some other lever for change than to invent one.

Restructuring or decentralization

This is the companion to delegation. Taking the Executive Agency initiative as an example, restructuring can be imposed on an organization in an attempt to make it more effective, through identifying separately the unique contribution it is to make. However, our research showed that this external restructuring was not always accompanied by internal change, either through increased delegation, clearer performance measurement or some other internal lever for change. *In these cases, the externally imposed change had little or no impact.* It is perhaps easier for restructuring to remain at the level of 'badge engineering' or simply changing the name over the door: to have any real impact, it has also to be accompanied by some internal changes which will have a real impact on the daily tasks people are asked to perform. If managers wish to *resist* change, it may be heartening for them to realize that they can dampen the effects of even apparently significant external change by continuing to operate as usual. For managers who wish to achieve change, they need to consider some of the alignment mechanisms set out in Figure 7.1.

Visibility

An important effect of much of the change has been to increase the external visibility of the organizations themselves, of what they are supposed to deliver and of named individuals who are in charge of that delivery. Thus many organizations have employed consultants to think about the image they project. Some, like the Central Office for Information, have a new logo and better presented reporting documents. All Executive Agencies now produce an Annual Report and all their Chief Executives are directly answerable to Parliament through the medium of appearances before Select Committees and direct answers to MPs' questions.

It is therefore clearer both to users and to observers that there are named public servants with responsibility for delivering a certain level of output. If used properly, this can be liberating on both sides. Managers can now expect a certain level of input to support required output: users can be more aware of the service to which they are entitled. The debate we are currently seeing in the National Health Service for example, becomes more open and better informed. All sides still use statistics for their own benefit: but the scope of debate is widened to stakeholders who previously might not have been privy to the necessary information in order to enable them to offer an opinion.

A power shift in the stakeholders

Just as managers and staff inside the organizations need to be persuaded to put their power behind the initiatives if they are to succeed, so other organizational stakeholders can have an impact on the changes. Customers or service users are important stakeholders and we have gone into some detail on how they might be made an effective force for change. Managers sometimes complain about how 'politics' stops them getting on with their jobs. Yet power shifts among different stakeholder groups is a fact of life in private sector organizations as well as public sector ones. One could argue that it is for managers to create alliances with the stakeholder groups who most closely support their view on change, rather than bemoaning their fate as the environment takes yet another swipe at them. Environmental issues are not always outside the control of those inside the organization: keen environmental awareness is certainly a key strategic weapon.

Stakeholder groups can be powerful and dangerous. A key public sector leader was ousted from the head of a charity during 1991 because he had underestimated the collective power of volunteers in a voluntary organization.

Choosing from the menu

It will be obvious to the reader that this list is not exhaustive. It is, however, the list which emerges most clearly from our research, to which we are sure that the reader will add ideas. We produced a map (Figure 7.1) to assist managers to analyse which external levers, outside their control, are being pulled and to make their choice of the appropriate internal levers to pull. The writings on change often polarize between those who recommend pulling internal levers and those who focus on the external levers. A clear conclusion from our research is that both need to be used: an external change may have no impact inside an organization at all and internal changes are often regarded as unnecessary and do not survive without an accompanying environmental change. The trick is, as ever, analysis and focus. Analyse the situation in which you find yourself and then focus hard on the two or three change mechanisms which have the best chance of success.

Our map also offers ideas on the best ways to resist change. Why? Surely public sector managers are public servants: their role is to serve and deliver, not to second-guess the political process. Chris Argyris (1987) wrote a very interesting essay on apparently inexplicable errors in strategic management by managers (in private sector organizations). One example was that already quoted above, of managers investing heavily in plant and machinery despite increasing amounts of evidence to show that this strategy was ineffective and that straightforward cost-cutting would have been more likely to ensure survival. Were the managers acting out of ignorance, or, more seriously, defending and covering up earlier mistakes, thus compounding earlier errors? Argyris talks of organizational defensive routines which are '... any routinized policies or actions that are intended to prevent the experience of embarrassment or threat and simultaneously make it unlikely that they can help to reduce the factors that caused the embarrassment or threat in the first place'. This is very similar to the defensive routine we outlined above, of turning mistakes into amusing and thus unthreatening anecdotes. Thus we cannot assume that managers are automatic units of change: they also need to buy the new ideas.

The outcome of defensive routines is that mixed messages become acceptable, so that no one gets hurt. For example, on decentralization versus control, senior managers will say, 'You are running the show' and then follow this with the all-important 'but ...'. The real issues, as Argyris says, become 'undiscussable and uninfluenceable' while managers and staff act as if this were not the case, therefore rendering even the undiscussability and uninfluenceability, undiscussable. These defensive routines lead people to feel helpless and cynical about changing them, a finding we would definitely endorse from our research.

But surely phrases like 'accountable management' and 'customer service' are about identifying clearly what is happening? Perhaps not. One of the clear themes from research across a broad spectrum, from Milgram's psychological experiments to Goldthorpe's *et al.*'s (1968) 'Affluent Worker' is that 'agencification' also carries dangers. In this discussion, we are considering the wider use of the term 'agency' as someone who carries out tasks on behalf of others, rather than the more specific type of organizational form, the Executive Agency. Of course, separating out an agency can identify responsibilities more clearly. But we have also to consider the nature of the responsibilities. Is there really a split between policy and execution, as the current reforms would have us believe? In private sector organizations, strategy is executed and then sales, or customer reaction, contribute heavily towards strategic change. Sometimes the changes may be made at Board level, after gathering market research data, or at the operational level, after reacting to a series of face-to-face customer views. If we accept that strategy or policy and execution can be separated, we also accept that new strategic stances *cannot* emerge from the bottom of organizations, through customer or user contact. Certainly it may disenfranchise the 'customers', whom the Government seem so keen to enfranchise between elections, in their relationship with public services, through the Citizens Charter.

So agencies may limit the opportunity for strategic change rooted in what customers really want.

Secondly, agencification may actually remove managers from responsibility for what they do. The Milgram experiments demonstrated clearly the degree to which becoming the agent of an 'expert' can dehumanize the process of dealing with other humans. More prosaically, it may divorce public sector managers from previous public sector values like equity and integrity. They have a clearly delimited role and deliver according to their circumscribed responsibilities. Recent seminars which we have run with public sector managers have been disappointing in that these managers have been unable to define any real difference between public and private sector management. We believe that there are and should be differences. Market research carried out by the Vehicle Inspectorate, for example, showed that their users want them to retain integrity and independence to a degree apparently not demanded from private sector companies. Norman Lewis, constitutional lawyer, a member of the Study of Parliament Group and Professor of Socio-Legal Studies at Sheffield University, echoes our concerns. He is worried about 'the ethics of the public sector and what separates it from the private sector'. Goldthorpe *et al.* also felt, more broadly, as Max Weber had concluded before him, that bureaucracy was the best means of ensuring fair distribution of resources. Goldthorpe *et al.* further noted that agencification meant losing the bureaucratic inclination to work.

So agencies may also limit responsibility to a degree which erodes public sector values still held in high regard by public sector users.

Thirdly, agencies are about enshrining the undiscussable. Some say that by depoliticizing public sector management, this enables managers to proceed with the task of service delivery, unencumbered by broader societal needs. Yet agencies are crucially not about depoliticization. Rather, they represent the market ideology rendered undiscussable. There is a political managerial vision rooted in conservatism. It embodies a view of markets and competition, of accountable units which may nonetheless lack authority and of a separation of politics and management. Yet 'good' management consists of all these elements. By accepting a shallower and narrower view of management, public sector managers are subliminally agreeing with a view of management which precludes them from adhering to previously cherished values.

So agencies may also render undiscussable the indisputable differences between excellent public, compared to private, sector management, or any version of management not deeply rooted in commercialism.

Is there an answer? No, but there is a proposition. Although we offer readers a map, Argyris' work simply heightens our concern, already stated, that managers should not follow steps 1–3 and then expect the same to happen as happened with, for example, the police force. Each manager should rather work creatively against the background of his or her specific organizational defence routines. This will change the implementation programme attempted and will alter the choice of change levers. Does the manager wish to work within the organizational defensive routines, for example, or to address the defensive routines straight on and challenge them as part of the change programme? The latter implies that the manager is aware enough to stand back from the organization and analyse the defensive routines. It also implies that more energy may be needed, a greater confluence of internal and external change levers.

Timing is extremely important. A mistake some managers seem to have made with Executive Agency status, for example, is to underplay it as a source of external influence or threat. This may have been pandering to the defensive routines of their organization, an attempt to ensure that no one feels threatened in order to implement some changes. What opportunity may have been lost to make even greater changes? The most successful Executive Agencies are those where Agency status has been presented, and used, as a source of real change, with early and symbolic examples of the changes it can bring.

Dilemmas

We have seen that managers in the public sector have been expected to change their behaviour in sometimes contradictory ways. Public services are not the same as businesses, but managers are often asked to behave in more 'business like' ways. This can produce serious value conflicts with which managers have to cope. Dilemmas thus continually present themselves. Some of them are representative of values changing in transition on the way to new operational forms and ways of working. Others may be of a more enduring quality.

The most important conflict is between maintaining equity of treatment and access to services and making a profit. Any unit which is engaged in trading, even if only in an internal market, is forced to concentrate on attracting revenue. Even Companies House has segmented its market and offers a higher quality and faster service to customers willing to pay a higher price. NHS units have been tempted to offer better access to patients who have 'purchasers' who are willing to offer higher prices or a better contract. Profit maximizing in public transport does not result in equal access to buses and trains.

Profit-making automatically drives out equity of treatment and yet managers are pushed in both directions at once. The only resolution of the dilemma would be to ensure that each potential 'customer' has equal access to funds. Choice would then be based only on preference and not ability to pay. Attractive suppliers could then survive at the expense of unattractive ones without detriment to groups of customers. However, such an approach would imply a rationing system based on some form of voucher whose value would be based on need. Rationing is at odds with a hands-off free market for services.

A second dilemma which public sector managers often express is between carrying out the task as well as possible and looking after the staff. Guaranteed employment at reasonable levels of income is often seen as contradictory to efficiency — if people cannot be sacked and have protected incomes, managers are powerless. This dilemma may be more easily resolved — a low-wage workforce ruled by fear of losing their jobs is probably not the best route to effective and efficient services. Good managers should be able to find other motivations than fear and should be able to achieve levels of productivity which justify decent incomes.

A third dilemma arises when the 'customer' is not a customer at all. Sometimes services are designed to exercise control or modify behaviour. To label offenders, for example, as 'customers' of the criminal justice system is clearly of limited usefulness. And yet many other areas of public service also have elements of control. The unemployment benefit system is designed, in part at least, to make sure that the labour market works well: that there are incentives for unemployed people to seek work. Medical services are partly designed to modify people's behaviour towards more healthy habits. These objectives are very different from the requirement to please customers enough for them to part with money in exchange for a service. In practice the dilemma may be rhetorical: the use of the term 'customer' may be used by the organization to remind itself that the people with whom it is dealing have certain rights. There are limits to the effectiveness of this linguistic trick: it might be more useful to build the management processes on the actual relationship between the organization and the people for whom it provides services. The rights which patients, pupils, offenders and others have are more complex than those of consumers and are often enshrined in law. The use of the 'customer' metaphor may distract service providers from service users' actual rights.

Internal dilemmas can also confuse managers: for example, how can collaborative working through 'flat' organizational structures be reconciled with a very hierarchical system of grades? How can a junior manager accept a good idea from a clerical officer without undermining her own status?

Any experimentation on the way towards a better service brings with it the risk of failing to implement exactly the legislation which provides the organization's rationale. Managers have constantly to make sure that their innovations do not break the laws or rules of the organization. One resolution of this dilemma is never to innovate. A more productive approach must be to ensure that good ideas are not stifled at birth or do not produce excessive personal risk for managers.

Discussions with managers reveal many such dilemmas. Some are unreconcilable and people follow a single value. However, the problem for the users of public services may be that changes in structure or rules of behaviour by public servants have unintended adverse consequences. The pursuit of profit might accidentally extinguish a right to equitable treatment. The pursuit of efficiency might so impoverish the workforce that service standards deteriorate. 'Freedom of choice' for one set of consumers may eliminate the rights of others to choose. The value dilemmas can cause managerial paralysis at a time of change. In some cases the paralysis may be beneficial. The real trick is for public sector managers to preserve *public* values while producing efficient and effective services.

Appendix 1 Summary of reforms

A brief history of the reforms in the public sector organizations in the book

1 The Civil Service.

1961: Plowden Report: introduced Public Expenditure Survey (PES).

1968: Fulton Report: Lord Fulton's suggestions included improving the quality and accountability of management in the civil service. However, the recommendations were resisted by senior civil servants and no fundamental changes occurred.

1970: Central Policy Review Staff appointed by Edward Heath.

1979: Election of Conservative government. 'The election of the Conservatives marked a turning point in the debate about efficiency and effectiveness in the civil service' (Drewry and Butcher, 1988).

1980: Sir Derek (now Lord) Rayner appointed to advise the Prime Minister and established the Efficiency Unit. Beginning of the 'Rayner scrutinies' of the business of government. One early result of Rayner's work was the setting up in 1980 of the Management Information System for Ministers (MINIS), which helped to reveal scope for economy and efficiency in the Department of Enviromnent.

1981: White Paper 'Efficiency in the Civil Service'.
Department of Health and Social Security: Traffic Study published in July 1981. (The 'traffic' being the flow of social security business between

local and regional offices and HQ.) One of its main recommendations was to give much greater autonomy to managers at the local level.

1982: Launch of Financial Management Initiative (FMI). The White Paper set out its three basic principles which were to 'Promote in each department an organization and a system in which managers at all levels have:

1. a clear view of their objectives, and means to assess and, wherever possible, measure outputs and performance in relation to those objectives;
2. well-defined responsibility for making the best use of their resources, including a critical scrutiny of output and value for money; and
3. the information (particulary about costs), the training and the access to expert advice that they need to exercise their responsibilities effectively.'

Department of Health and Social Security: January 1982: report from Price Waterhouse Associates entitled 'Development of a Budgetary control System for the Administration Vote'. Price Waterhouse concluded that 'the introduction of a system of budgetary control over departmental administrative costs is both justifiable and desirable'.

1983: Sir Robin Ibbs succeeds Rayner at the Efficiency Unit.

The system of budgetary control envisaged in the FMI was first introduced into the Department of Health and Social Security's Regional Organization in financial year 1983/84.

1988: 'Management in Government: The Next Steps' published (also known as the Ibbs report) on the establishment of Executive Agencies.

Next Steps Unit established to manage the creation of Executive Agencies.

By July 1991 52 Agencies had been set up, employing 211 560 people.

Next Steps – Executive Agencies Established as of 11 July 1991

	Employees
Building Reasearch Establishment	690
Cadw (Welsh Historic Monuments)	220
Central Office of Information[1]	680
Chemical Veterinary Laboratory	600

Chemical and Biological Defence Establishment[2]	560
Civil Service College	230
Companies House	1 100
Defence Research Agency	11 700
Directorate General of Defence Accounts[2]	2 150
Driver and Vehicle Licensing Agency	5 250
Driving Standards Agency	2 100
Employment Service	34 500
Forensic Science Service	600
Historic Royal Palaces	340
Historic Scotland	610
HMSO[1]	3 250
Hydrographic Office[2]	850
Insolvency Service	1 500
Intervention Board	940
Laboratory of the Government Chemist	340
Land Registry	10 050
Medicines Control Agency	310
Meteorological Office	2 300
Military Survey[2]	800
National Engineering Laboratory	380
National Physical Laboratory	830
National Weights and Measures Laboratory	40
Natural Resources Institute	420
NHS Estates	120
Occupational Health Service	100
Ordnance Survey	2 450
Patent Office	1 200
Queen Elizabeth II Conference Centre	70
Radiocommunications Agency	500
RAF Maintenance[2]	5 700
Rate Collection Agency (Northern Ireland)	270
Recruitment and Assessment Services Agency	280
Registers of Scotland	1 200
Royal Mint[1]	1 050
Scottish Fisheries Protection Agency	200
Service Children's Schools (North West Europe)[2]	1 000
Social Security Agency (Northern Ireland)	5 000
Social Security Benefits Agency	65 600
Social Security Contributions Agency	7 200
Social Security Information Technology Services Agency	3 600
Social Security Resettlement Agency	470
Training & Employment Agency (Northern Ireland)	1 700

UK Passport Agency	1 200
Vehicle Certification Agency	80
Vehicle Inspectorate[1]	1 850
Veterinary Medicines Directorate	70
Warren Spring Laboratory	310
52 in number	184 560
Customs & Excise[3] (30 Executive Units)	27 000
	211 560

---

[1] Trading Funds
[2] Defence Support Agency. Figure does not include service personnel.
[3] Roving towards full operation on Next Steps lines following publication of Framework Documents. Staffing Figures are rounded and based on .Civil Service staff in post (FTE) 1 April 1991.

At that time a further 26 were under consideration with 17 700 employees as well as the Inland Revenue.

2   Education

1976:   James Callaghan Ruskin College speech renewed the education debate.

1980:   Education Act. Strengthened parental rights by encouraging choice and involvement in schools. Introduced Planned Admission Limits.

1981:   Solihull became the first LEA to make a serious attempt at decentralizing its education authority.
   Education Act encouraged the integration of pupils with special needs into mainstream schools.

1986:   Education Act (II) provided for the governing bodies of schools to have discretion over budgets for certain goods and services. This came into effect from September 1987, but in many cases it only served to formalize existing practices. It aslo increased the influence of parents and business community; schools had to publish details of costs incurred and to pay attention to marketing.

April 1987:   Kent introduced a pilot scheme of local financial management in selected schools, the number of which grew rapidly.

1988:   Education Reform Act stipulated that every local education authority (with the exception of ILEA) should submit its own scheme and proposals for a system of Local Management of Schools (LMS). Under LMS, after financial delegation to the schools, LEAs were required to withdraw to a 'policing' and advisory role and this meant losing many of powers to the governing bodies of schools. Also provided for schools to 'opt out' of local authority control and the introduction of city technology colleges (CTCs).

3   London Transport

1980:   reorganization created eight bus districts, each with it own general manager. Garbutt (1985) commented that: 'the stated purposes of the changes was to clarify lines of management and financial control, and delegate more decision-making to local managements with a fuller knowledge of conditions in their areas'.

1982:   Budgets began to be prepared in the districts, followed by a gradual devolvement of work from HQ.

1984:   London Regional Transport Act transferred responsibility for London Transport from the GLC to the government. Also, a requirement of the Act was to establish seperate companies to run the underground and buses:

1985:   London Buses Limited (LBL) was established.
   Transport Act (1985) made provision for the eventual deregulation followed by the privatization of London Regional Transport. Bus services deregulated outside Greater London.

1986:   The remaining bus districts have many of the functional ingredients of a business.

1986:   Establishment of the subsidiary bus companies within LBL on 1 April.

4   Northamptonshire Police Authority

1964:   Police Act encouraged cost-effectiveness.

1980–1:   Theories about police management were developing at the police staff college at Bramshill, mainly promoted by Kenneth Newman. The emphasis was on devolved management generally.

1981: Scarman Report on Brixton disorders encouraged chief constables to start consultation arrangements.

1982: Maurice Buck, a Bramshill alumnus, appointed Chief Constable in Northamptonshire. Reformed the force around the concept of 'Policing by Objectives' (PBO) was developed in the United States by Lubans and Edgar and was adopted for the police from the Management by Objectives approach. Thibault, Lynch and McBride (1985) described it as a system for 'accountability, forward planning and fiscal organization'.

Horton and Smith (1988) describes the aims of PBO: 'It (PBO) seeks to promote dynamism within the organisation, it devolves responsibility for setting and working towards objectives to managers at each level of the hierarchy, and it encourages participation and feed-back from the bottom level of the organisation.'

1983: 1 January: PBO was introduced in Northamptonshire and is still in place. Although Buck has gone, his successor, David O'Dowd, has taken decentralization further with budgetary devolvement.

Home Office circular issued, entitled Manpower, Effectiveness and Efficiency in the Police Service'. Encouraged budgetary devolution.

Appendix 2 Public sector agency research project

Telephone questionnaire

Introduction

I am carrying out research for Liz Mellon of the London Business School. We are examining the impact of the shift to agency status in Public sector organizations. I have been given your name by _____ and would like to ask you a series of questions over the telephone which should take about 30 minutes. My questions broadly cover the areas of financial control, where and how decisions are made and customer service. (Either arrange appointment or launch into questions)

Interview details

Agency ....

Name ....

Title ....

What are your main areas of responsibility?

To which post do you report?

Do you control any budgets? (brief list, detail later)

General

1   In your view what were the motivations for the agency initiative?
(Aim to establish their personal perception.)
(prompt – better financial control
              – political ideas about bureaucracy
              – part of government wide changes
              – government concern to get better service delivery to users
              – concern to cut the number of civil servants
              – Treasury concern to cut costs)

2   To what degree has decision making been pushed down your
organization? Can you give me examples?
(Aim – build broad picture of real changes linked to agency status.)
(prompt – capital expenditure
              – hire and fire
              – process methods
              – resource allocation
              – promotion
              – level of service provided)

3   (a) Has the degree of delegation changed within the organization in
practice? What authority or decisions are now delegated that were
not previously?
(Aim – establish extent to which decentralization permeates the
whole organization as opposed to stopping at the CEO. Look for
changed relationship to the centre.)
(b) Does the theory differ from the practice? (Factual – if there are rules
what are they, get copies if possible.)

Budgets

4   I would like to understand how the budget is made up and adminis-
tered and whether the agency initiative has made a difference to this
process. (Factual – what are the rules, is the basis incremental or zero
based, do theory and practice differ.)
What part to you play in setting the following:

- overall divisional expenditure
- service headings
- detailed estimates under subjective headings

What part do you play in managing spending within set budgets?

5 I would like to know what happens when there are budget overspends or underspends. (Factual – look for theory vs practice, effects of agency initiative.)

- who checks on variances?
- what scope is there for virement and who makes these decisions?
- is there scope for retaining savings into the next year or is strict annuality observed? Are budgets based on gross costs or unit costs?

6 What changes would make your job more effective? (Opinion.)

- where budget decisions are made
- how budgets are planned
- scope for virement and budget carry over

Accountability

7 I am interested in what other monitoring is carried out. (Check on changes with agency status.)

- what other data are collected regularly, by whom?
- how is that information used? (Attitude – useful management tool or custodial.)
- on what measures is your own division's performance judged?
- what part do you play in setting objectives and performance measures for yourself and those below you?

Customer service

8 I am interested in the effect of the change to agency status on the service that you deliver.

- how do you measure service delivery (Look for outcome measures vs output measures, service quality vs process efficiency.)
- have any surveys/studies been done on the effects of decentralization on clients? (Can we have copies?)

- how are decisions made on changes to your current services? (e.g. dropping a service, switching resources from one service to another)
- how are decisions made on provision of new services outside your statutory duties?

Personnel

9 Who sets staffing levels: (What part do personnel play?)

- overall for the agency?
- for your division?

10 What criteria are used for these decisions?

11 Where is recruitment carried out for each level of staff?

12 Who makes decisions on promotion?

13 Has the switch to agency status changed staff roles?

- have staff (clerks, EOs, HEOs etc.) been asked to take on increased responsibilities?
- has staff behaviour changed?
- has pay been increased for enhanced responsibilities?

Further comments

14 Would you make any further comments on the switch to agency status? In particular would you like to see any further change in your own role. (Scope of responsibility/accountability, degree of flexibility.)

References

Argyris, C. (1987) First- and second-order errors in managing strategic change: the role of organizational defensive routines. In A. Pettigrew (ed) *The Management of Strategic Change*, Oxford: Blackwell

Bishop, M. and Kay, J. (1988) *Does Privatization Work? Lessons from the UK.* London: London Business School

Bowles, C. (1983) Marketing Public Transport. *Local Government Policy Making*, **10**, 2

Carlzon, J. (1990) *Moments of Truth.* New York: Harper and Row

Chisnall, P. M. (1986) *Marketing Research* (3rd edn) London: McGraw-Hill

Cmnd 8616 (1982) *Efficiency and Effectiveness in the Civil Service.* London: HMSO

Davies, J. and Snell, R. (1986) *The Process of Disillusionment: A Block to Creativity in Managers.* Lancaster: Lancaster University

Downes, P. (ed) (1988) *Local Financial Management in Schools.* Oxford: Basil Blackwell

Drewry, G. and Butcher, T. (1988) *The Civil Service Today.* Oxford: Basil Blackwell

Edwardes, M. (1984) *Back From the Brink.* London: Pan

Efficiency Unit (1988) *Management in Government: the Next Steps.* London: HMSO

Efficiency Unit (1991) *Making the Most of Next Steps.* London: HMSO

Flynn, N. and Common, R. (1990) *Contracting for Community Care.* London: Department of Health

Furze, A. (1986) What the opinion surveys say about local government. *Local Government Policy Making*, **13**, 2

Garbutt, P. (1985) *London Transport and the Politicians.* Shepperton: Ian Allan

Goldthorpe, J. H., Lockwood, D., Bechhofer, F. and Platt, J. (1968) *The Affluent Worker.* Cambridge: Cambridge University Press

Grant, R. M. (1987) Business strategy and strategy change in a hostile environment: failure and success among British cutlery producers. In A. Pettigrew (ed) *The Management of Strategic Change.* Oxford: Blackwell

Greiner, L. E. and Schein, V. E. (1988) *Power and Organisation Development.* London: Addison Wesley

Griffiths, R. (1988) *Community Care.* London: HMSO

Hampden-Turner, C. (1990) *Corporate Culture: From Vicious to Virtuous Circles.* London: Economist Books

Handy, C. (1989) *The Age of Unreason*. London: Century Hutchinson

Harrison, A. J. (1989) *The Control of Public Expenditure 1979–1989*. Newbury: Policy Journals.

Hood, C. and Jones, G. W. (1990) *Treasury and Civil Service Select Committee 8th Report*, 'Progress in the Next Steps Initiative', Appendix 6.

Horton, C. and Smith, D. (1988) *Evaluating Police Work*. London: Policy Studies Institute

International Monetary Fund (1988) 'Input controls in the public sector: what does economic theory offer?', prepared by David Heymann, *IMF Working Paper*, WP/88/59

Jay, A. (1972) *Corporation Man*. Harmondsworth: Penguin

Keleher, R. and Cole, C. (1989) Marketing: is it really relevant to the NHS? *Health Services Management*, February 1989.

Kennedy, A. and Deal, T. (1982) *Corporate Cultures*. London: Addison Wesley

Levin, H. M. (1989) 'The theory of choice as applied to education. Stanford University: Centre for Educational Research at Stanford, *Occasional Paper* 89-CERAS-10

Lovelock, C. H., Lewin, G., Day, G. S. and Bateson, J. E. G. (1987). *Marketing Public Transit*. New York: Praegar.

Lubans, V. A. and Edgar, J. M. (1979) *Policing By Objectives*. Hartford, Connecticut. Social Development Corporation

Mintzberg, H. (1983) *Structure in Fives: Designing Effective Organisations*. New Jersey: Prentice Hall

Pettigrew, A. (ed) (1987) *The Management of Strategic Change*. Oxford: Blackwell

Pollitt, C., Harrison, S., Hunter, D. J. and Marnoch, G. (1988) General management in the NHS: the initial impact 1983–88. *Public Administration*, **66**, 2

Thibault, E. A., Lynch, L. M. and McBride, R. B. (1985) *Proactive Police Management*. New Jersey: Prentice-Hall

Walsh, K. (1991) *Competitive Tendering for Local Authority Services: Initial Experiences*. London: HMSO

White, P. R. (1986) *Public Transport: Its Planning, Management and Operation* (2nd edn). London: Hutchinson

Young, K. and Hadley, R. (1990) *Creating a Responsive Public Service*. Hemel Hempstead: Harvester-Wheatsheaf

Index